Real World

Colouring Book

For Advanced Users & Adults

50 Images

Created From Real Life Photos
For You To Colour As You Please.

ISBN 978-0-359-82336-9

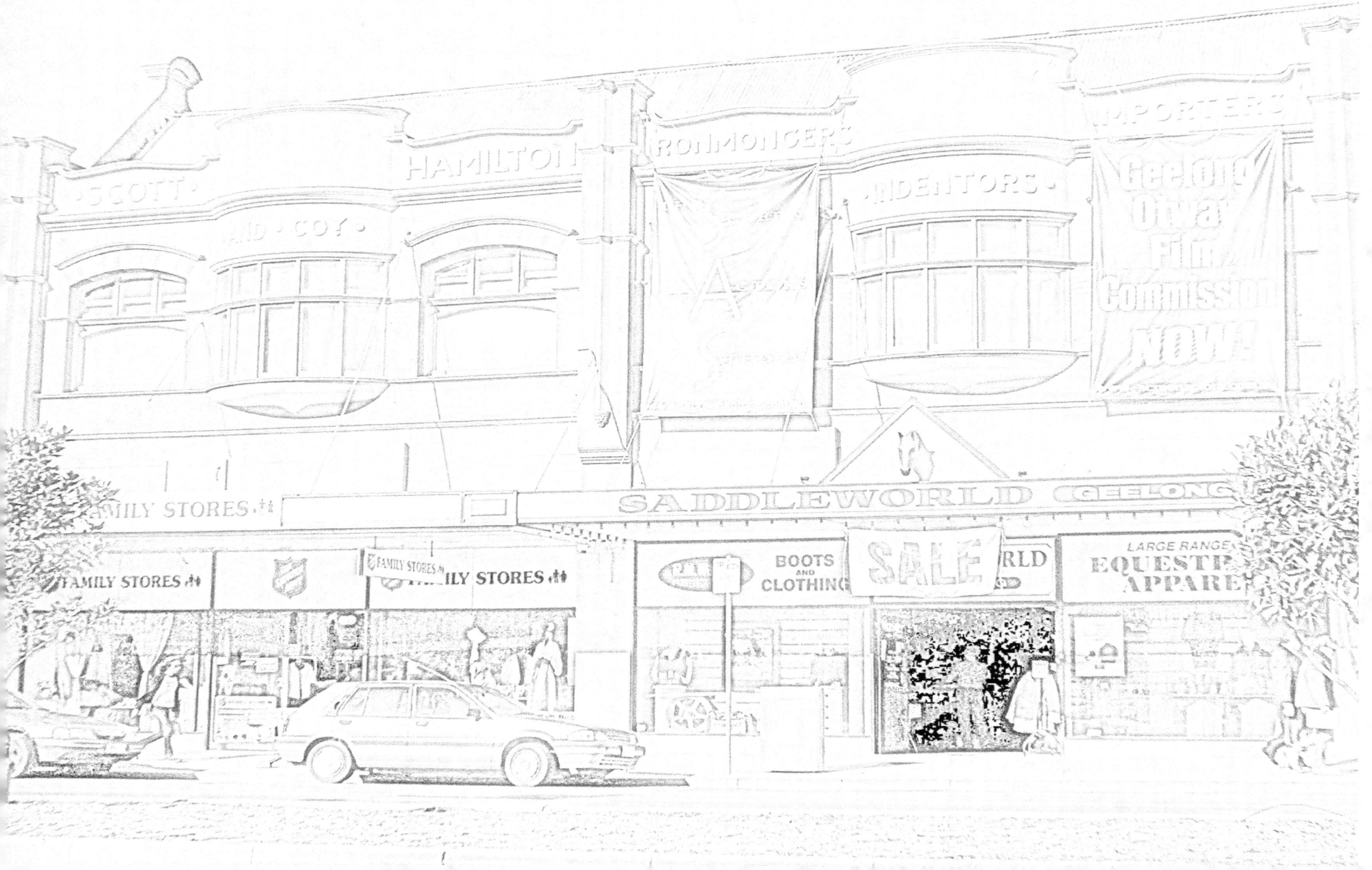
SCOTT
HAMILTON
AND COY
IRONMONGERS
INDENTORS
IMPORTERS
Geelong Otway Film Commission NOW!
SADDLEWORLD GEELONG
FAMILY STORES
BOOTS AND CLOTHING
SALE
LARGE RANGE
EQUESTR APPARE

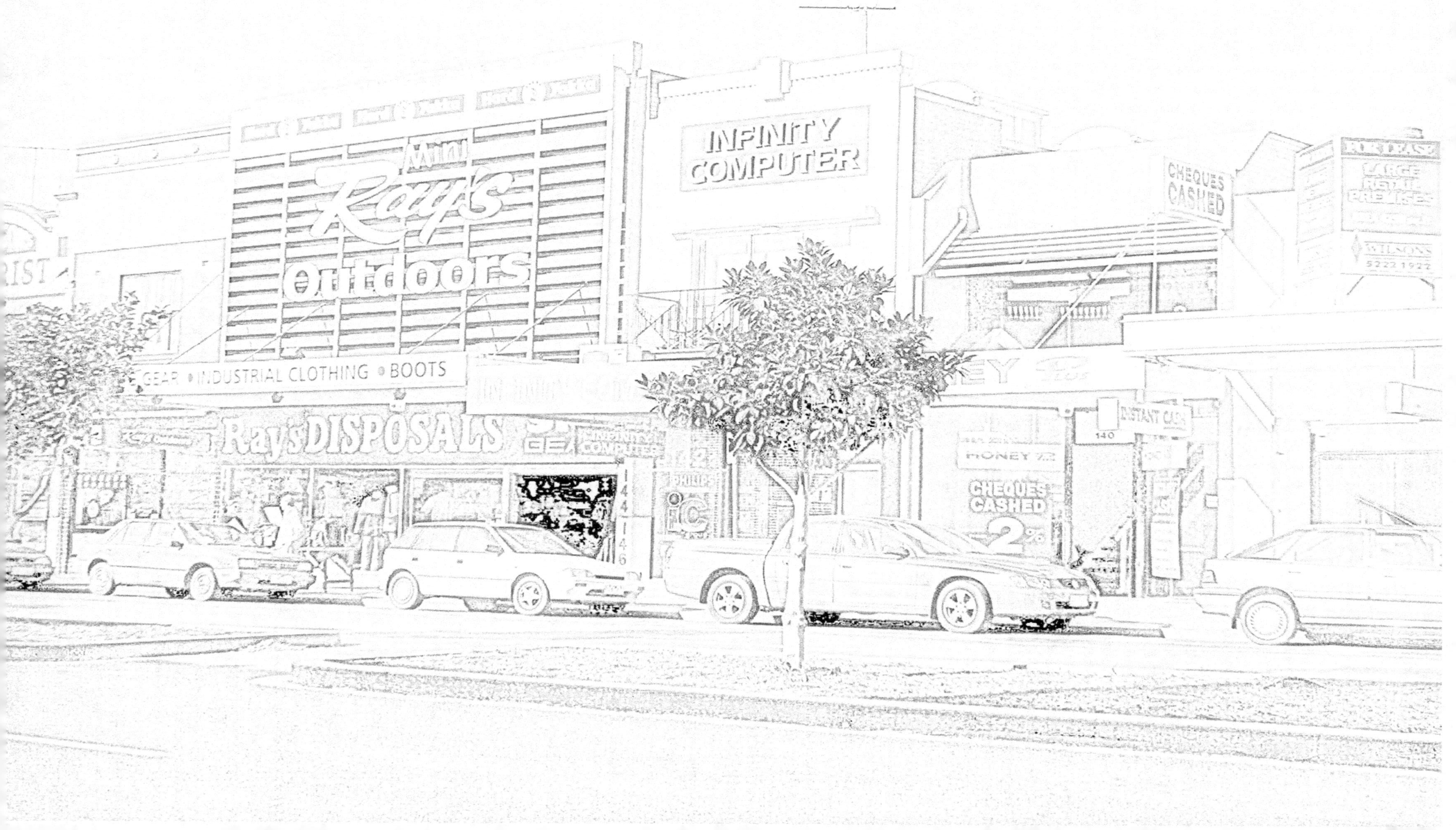

INFINITY
COMPUTER
Mini
Ray's
Outdoors
GEAR • INDUSTRIAL CLOTHING • BOOTS
Ray's DISPOSALS
CHEQUES
CASHED
CHEQUES
CASHED
2%
INSTANT CASH
140
144
146
FOR LEASE
LARGE
RETAIL
PREMISES
WILSONS
5222 1922

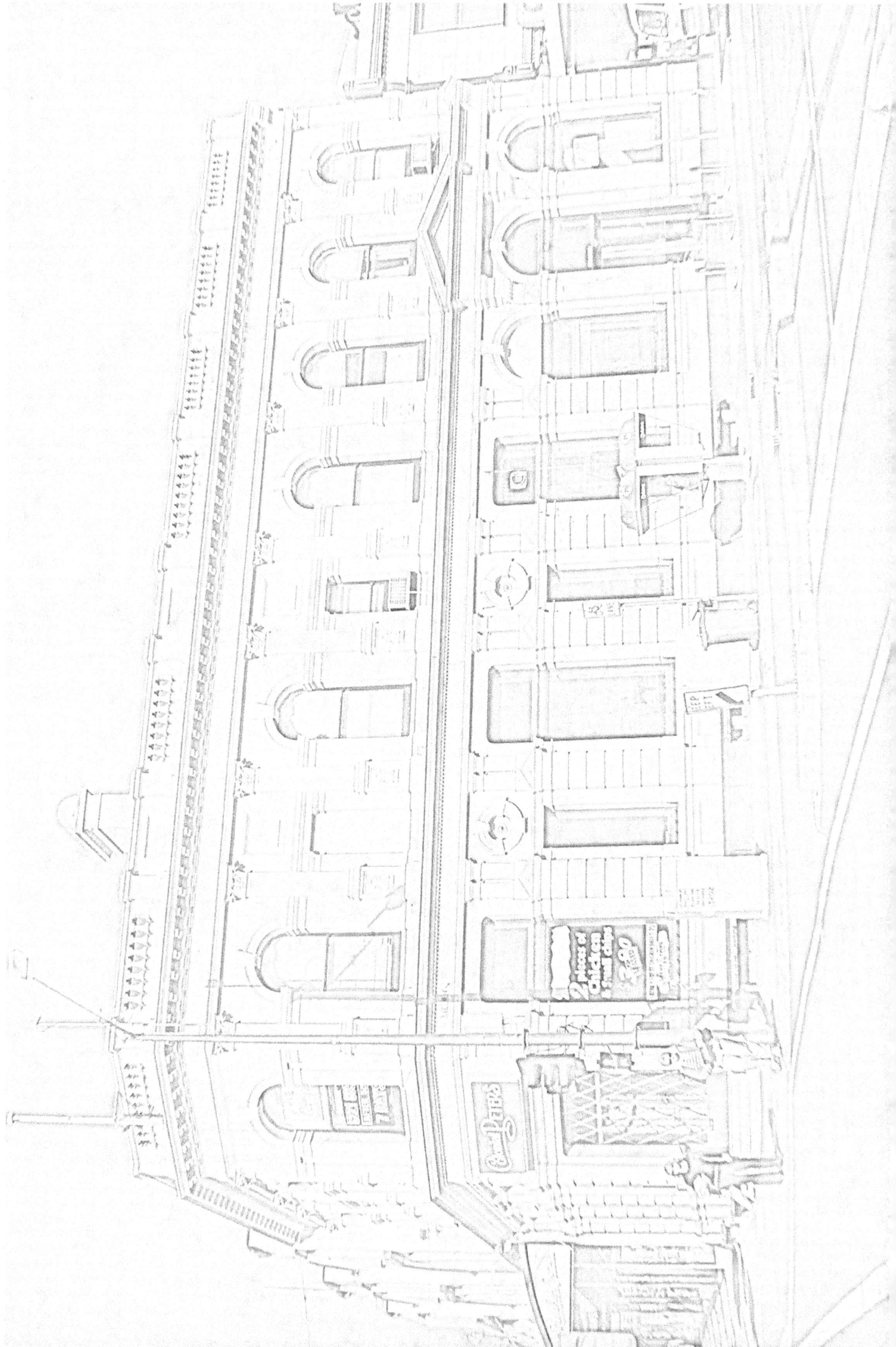

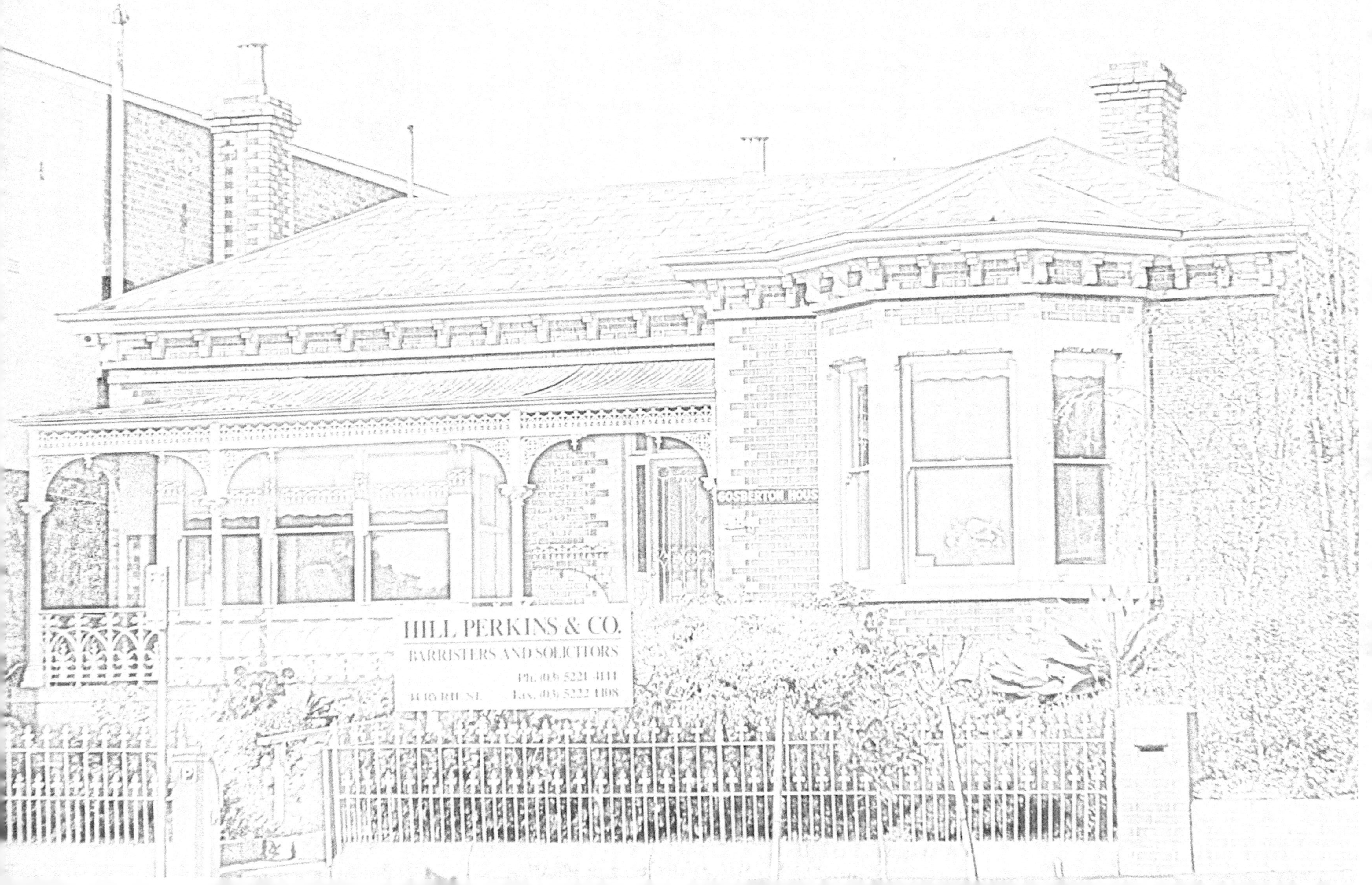
GOSBERTON HOUS
HILL PERKINS & CO.
BARRISTERS AND SOLICITORS
Ph. (03) 5221 4111
Fax. (03) 5222 1108

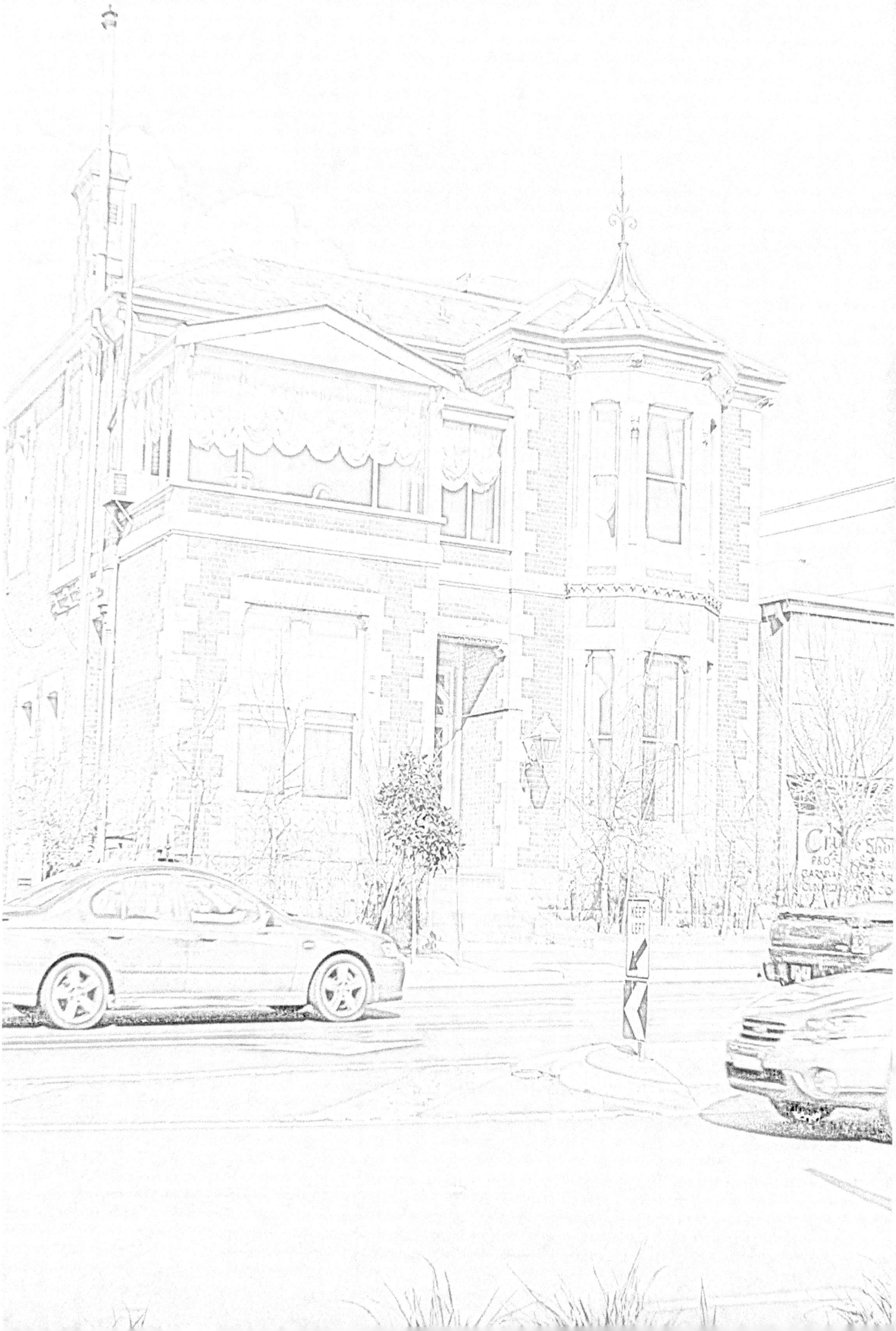
KEEP LEFT

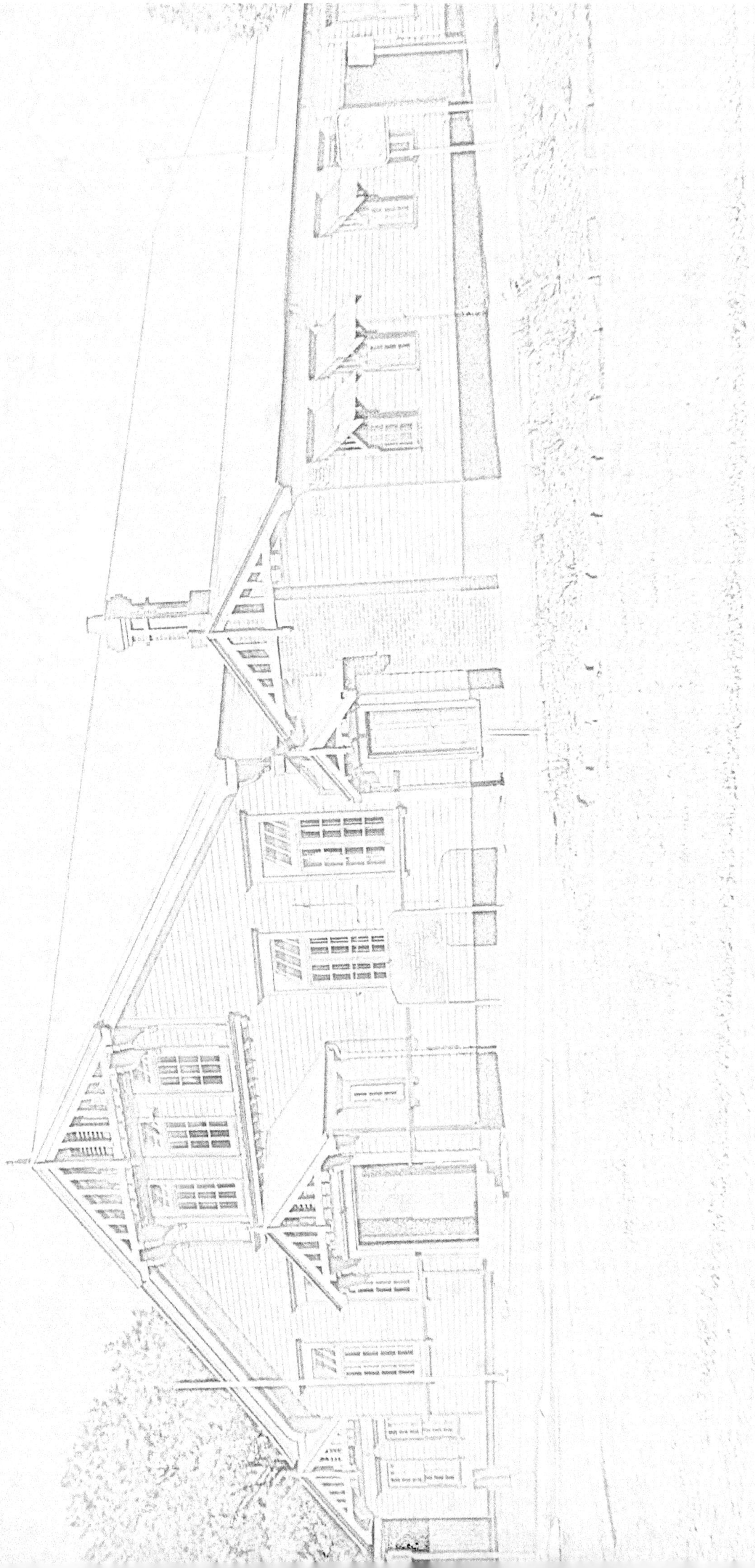

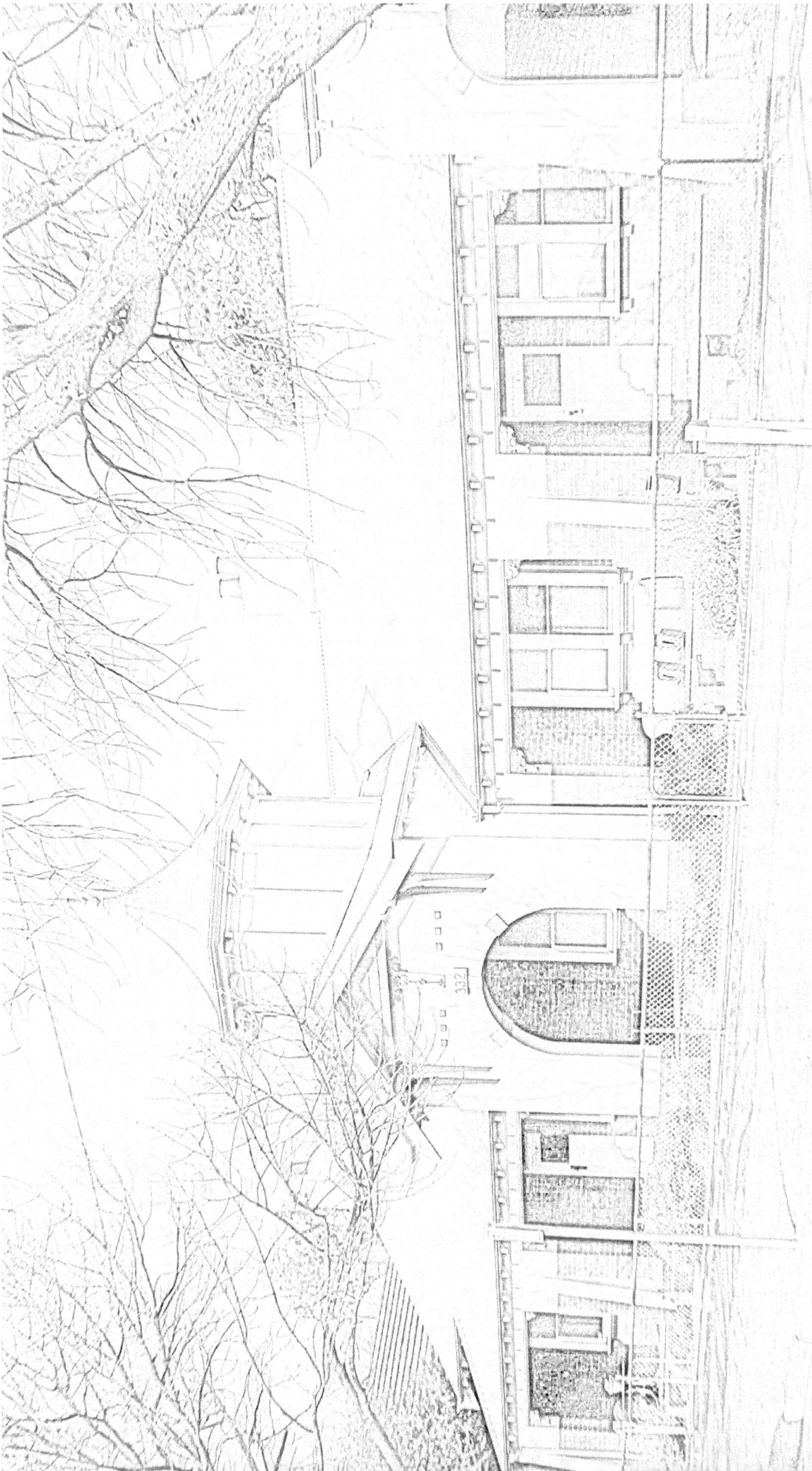
332

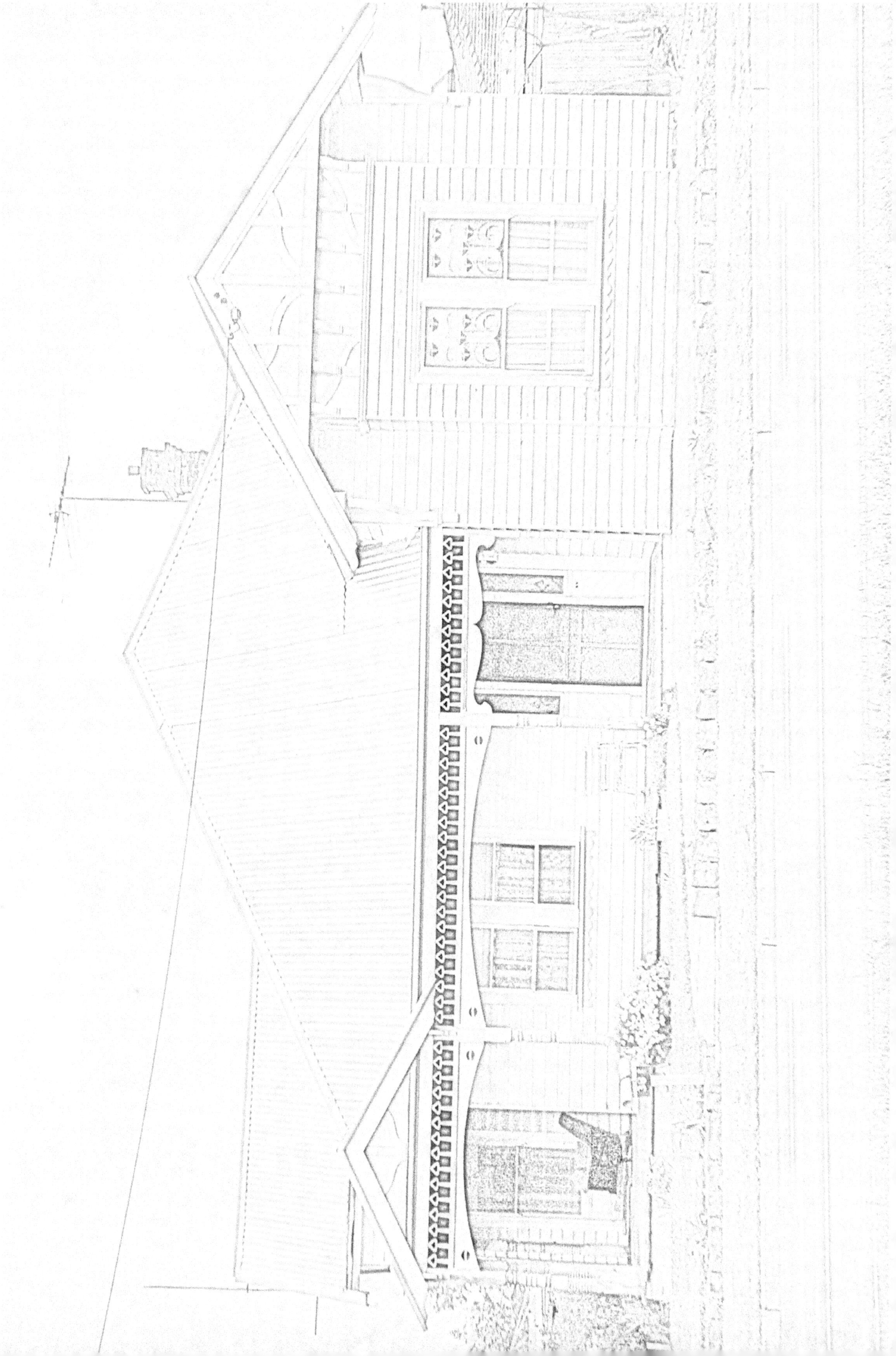

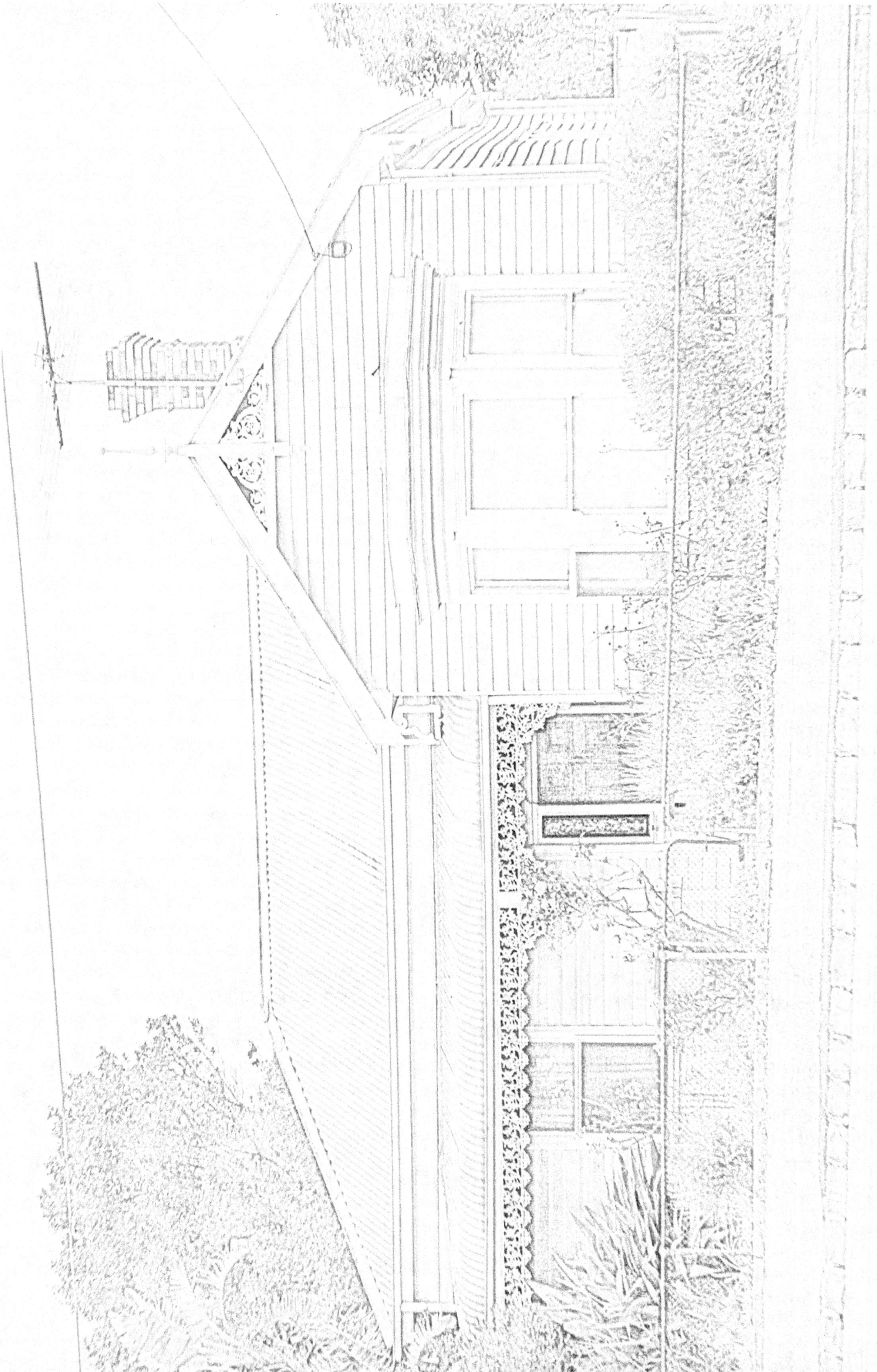

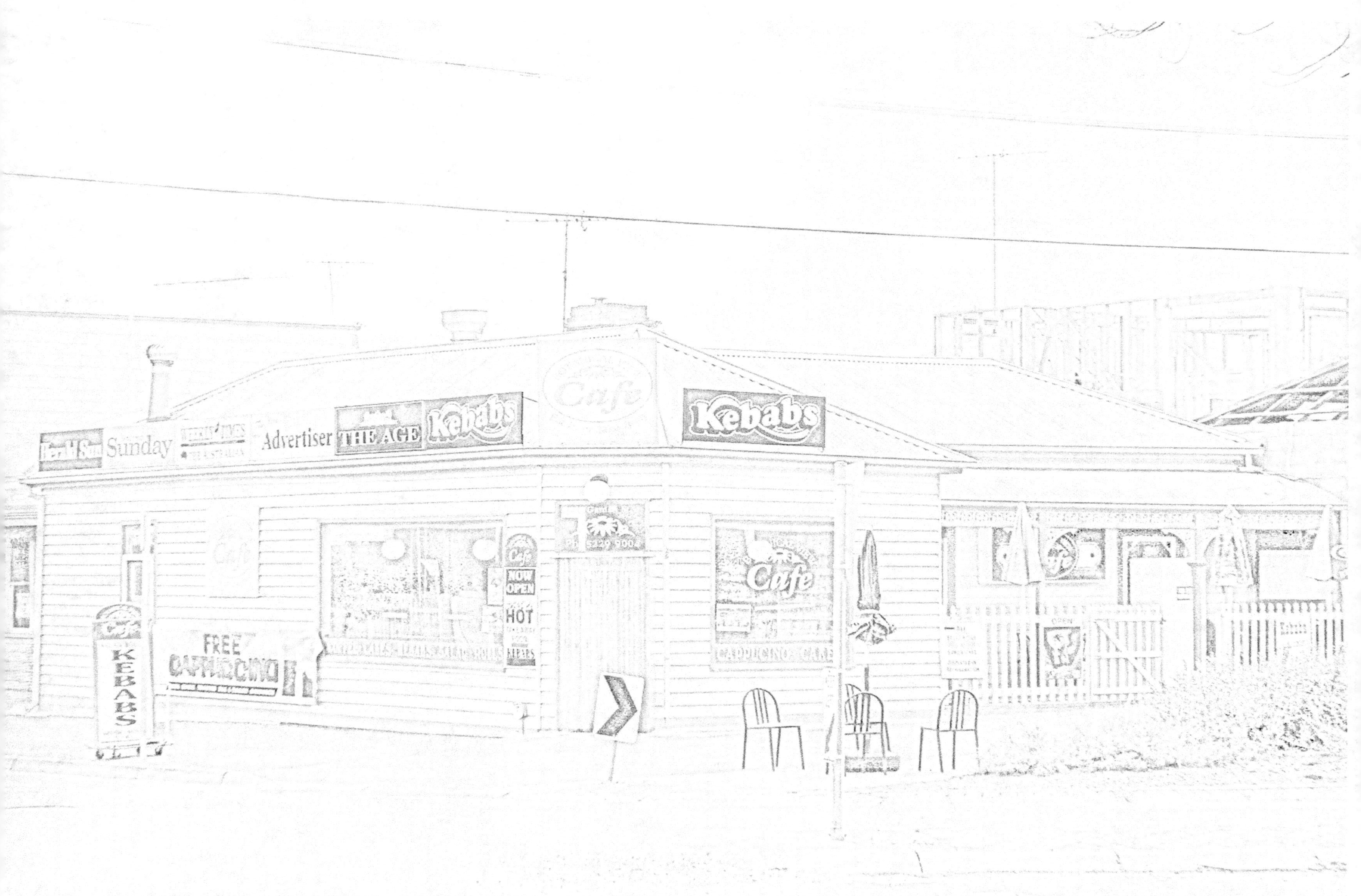
Sunday
Advertiser
THE AGE
Kebabs
Cafe
Kebabs
NOW OPEN
HOT
Cafe
CAPPUCINO
FREE
CAPPUCCINO
KEBABS

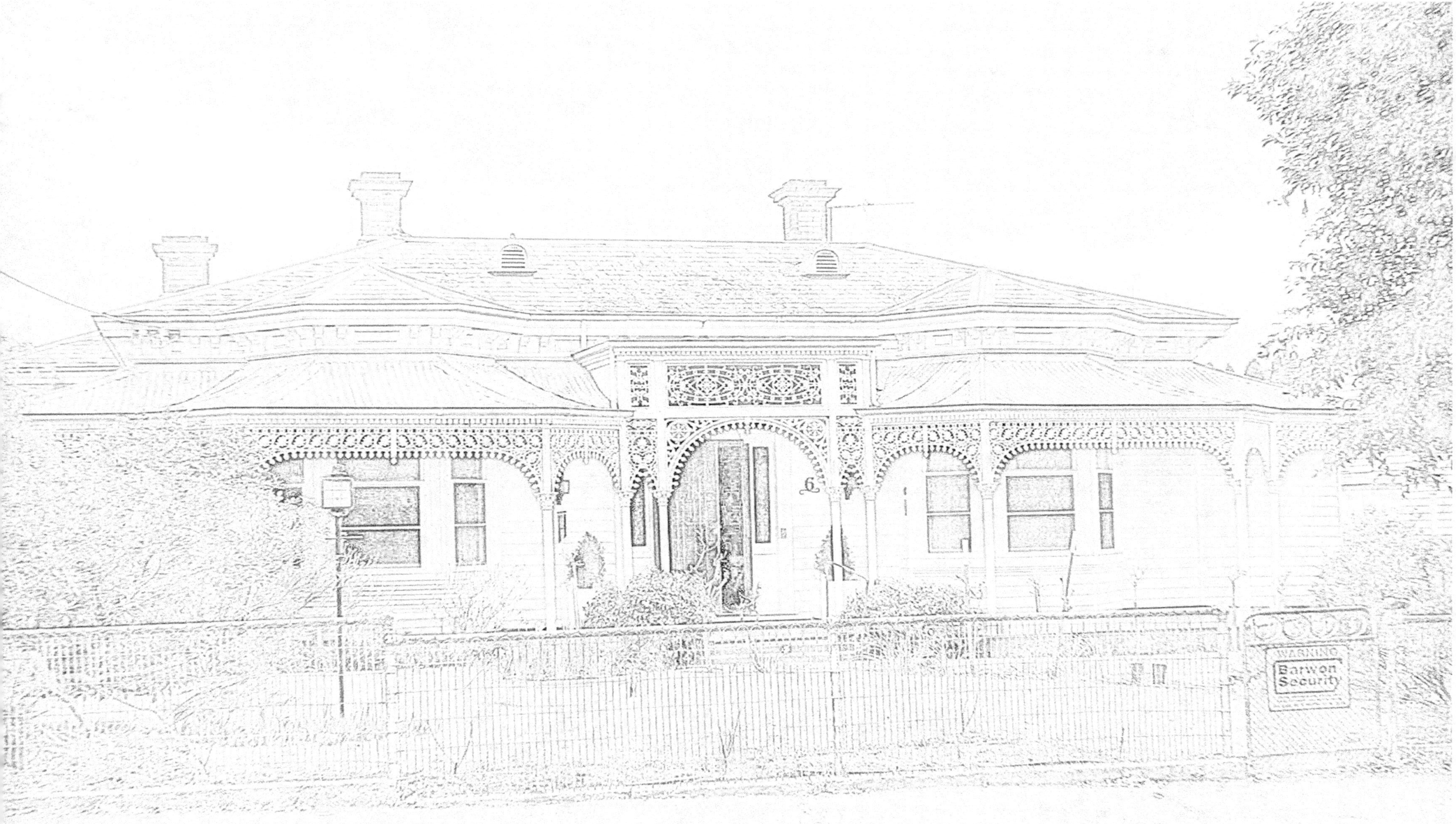
6
WARNING
Barwon Security

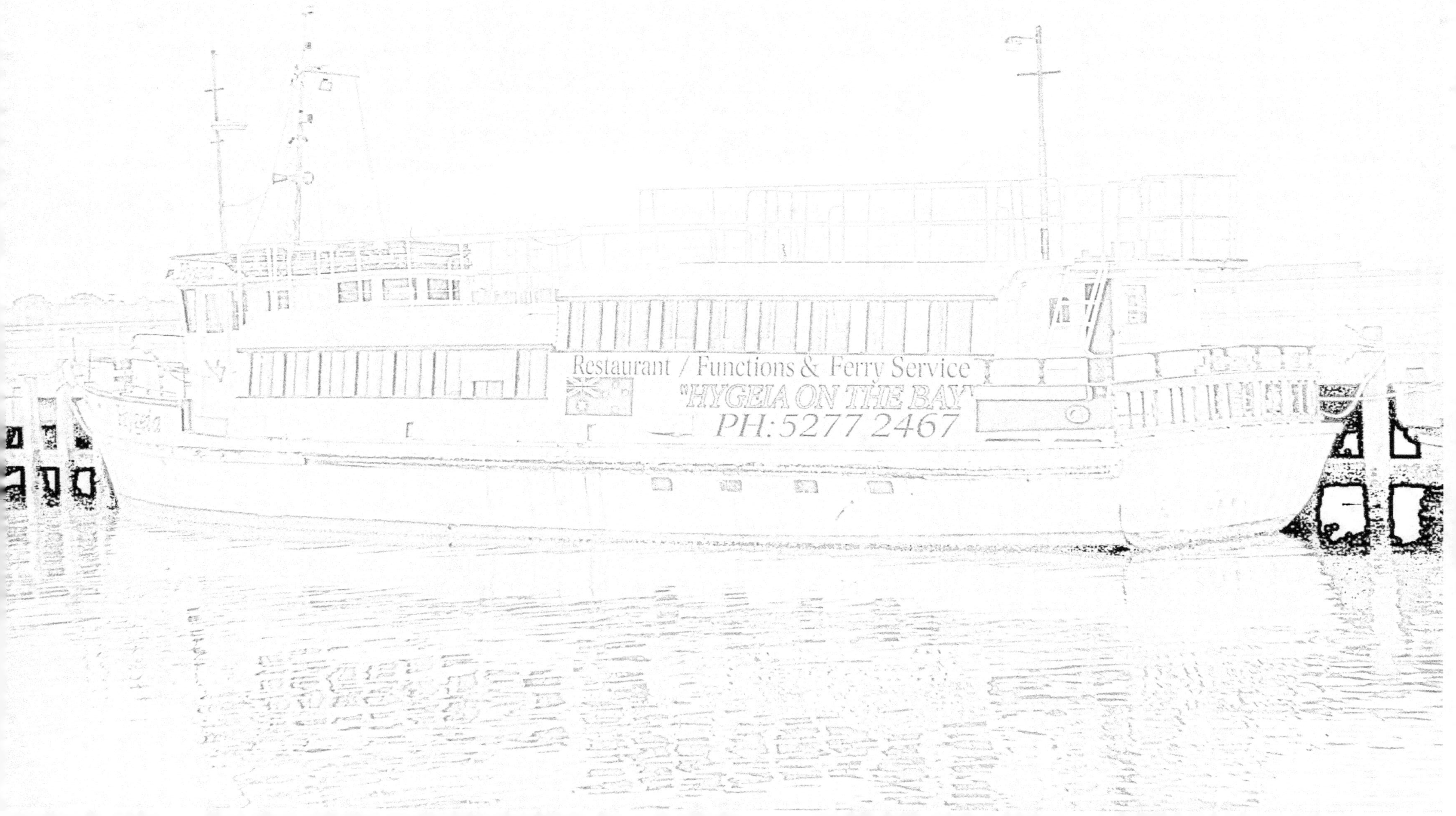
Restaurant / Functions & Ferry Service
"HYGEIA ON THE BAY"
PH: 5277 2467

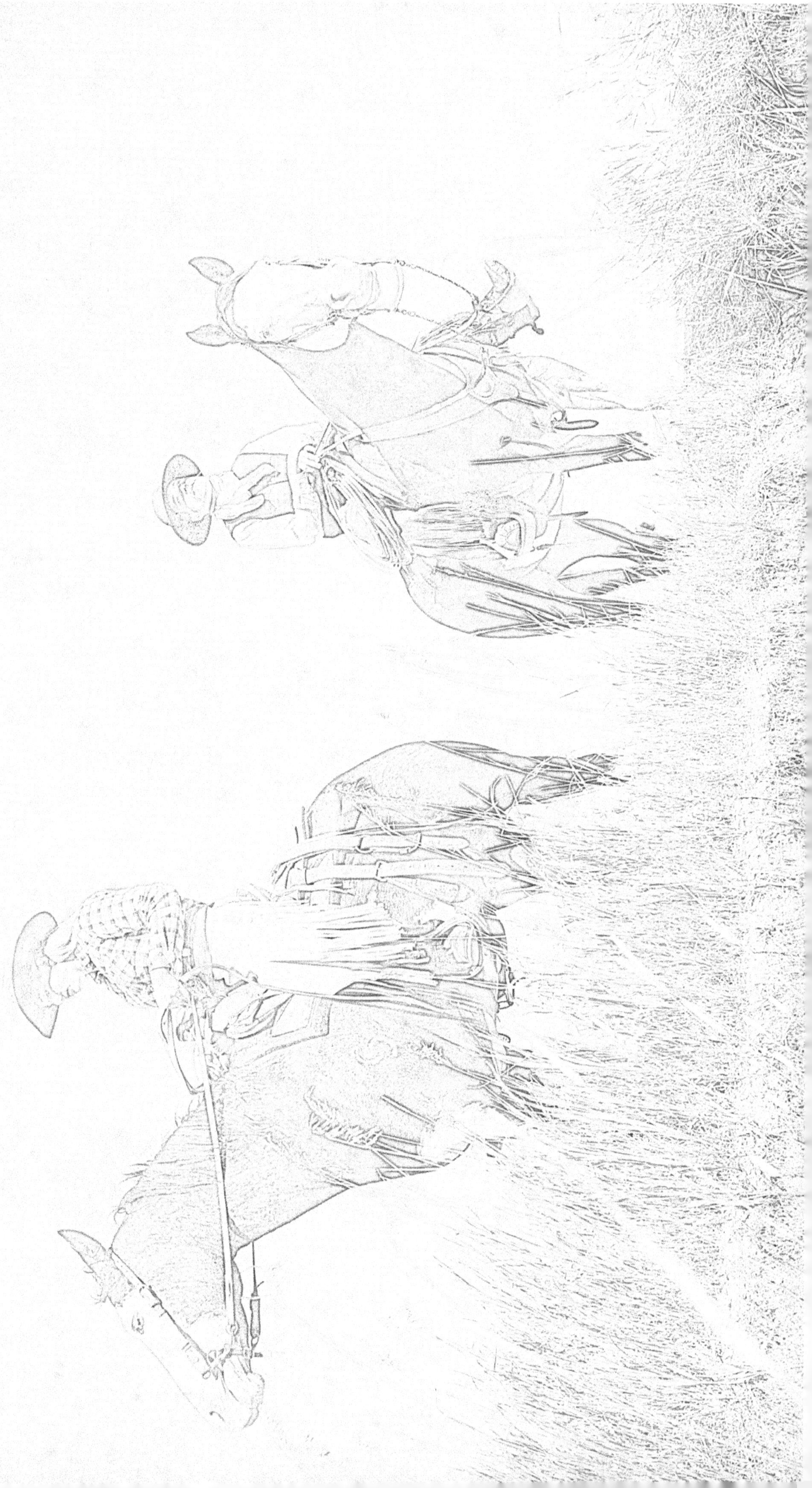

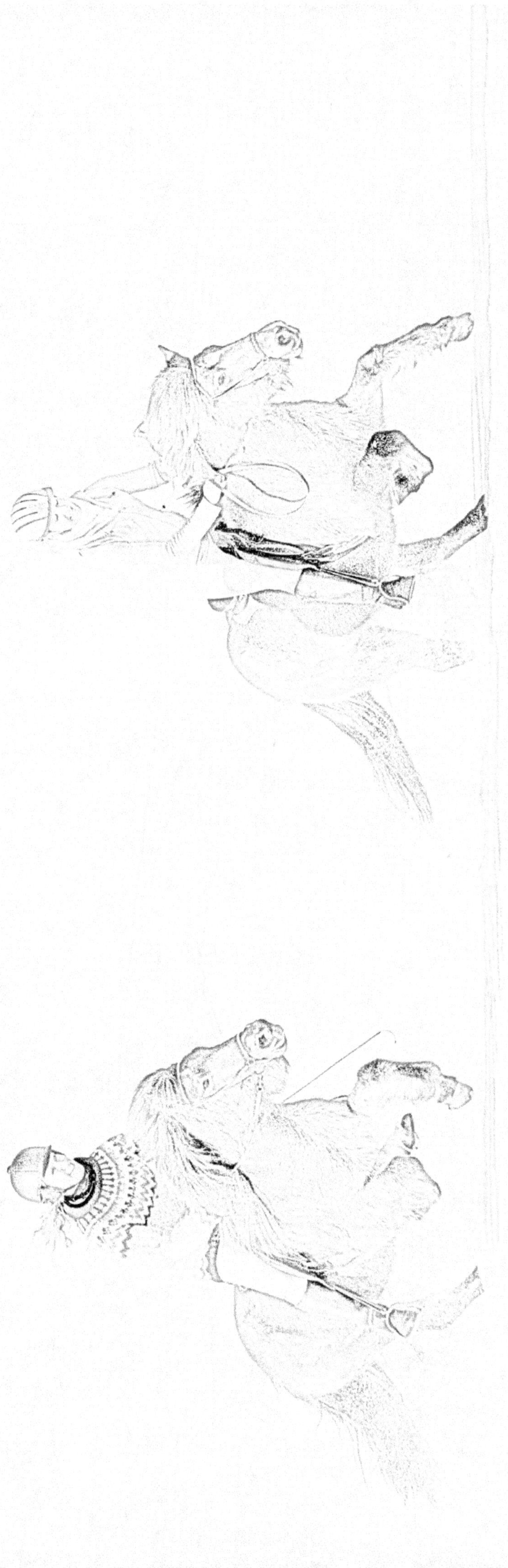

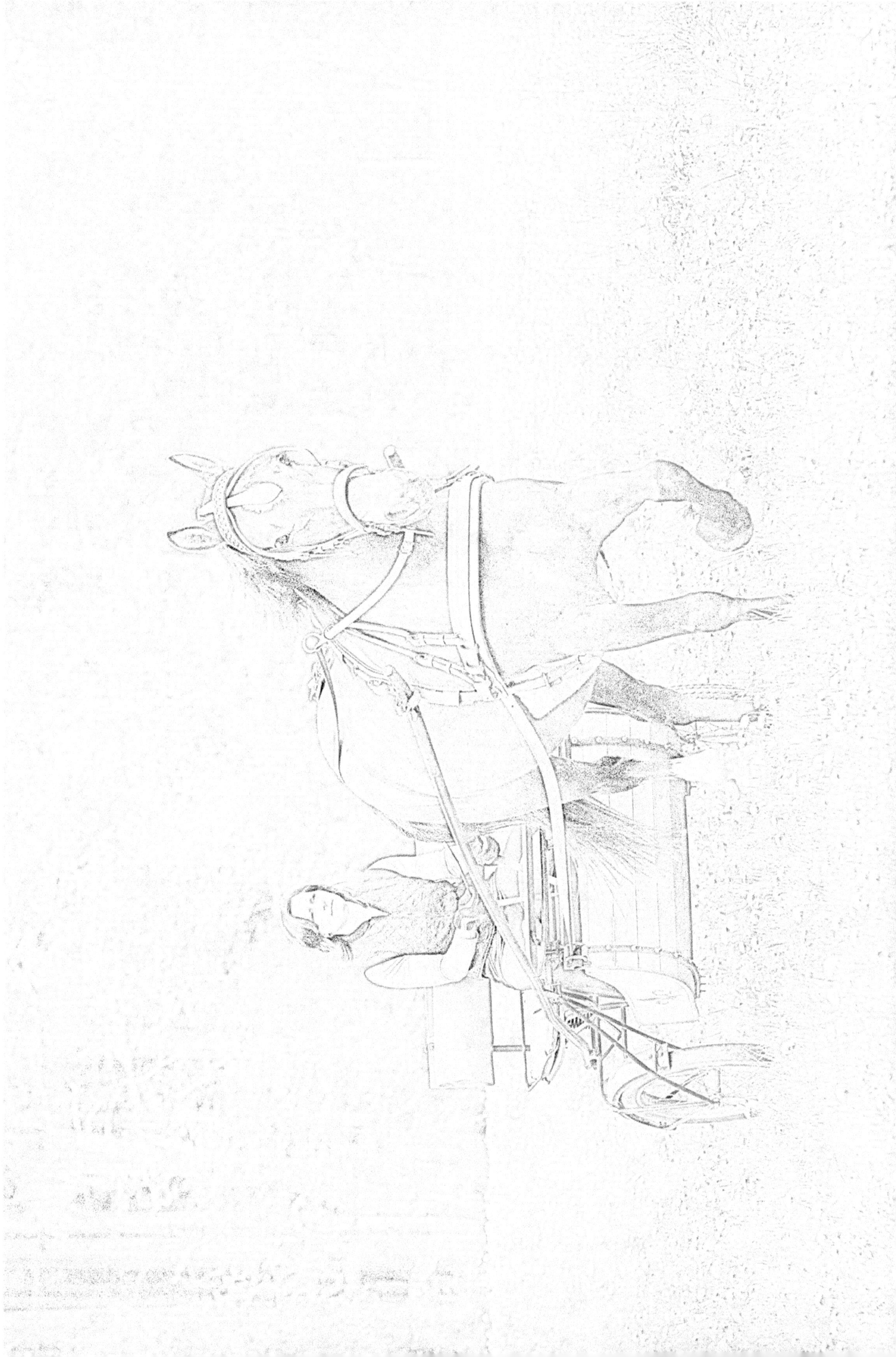

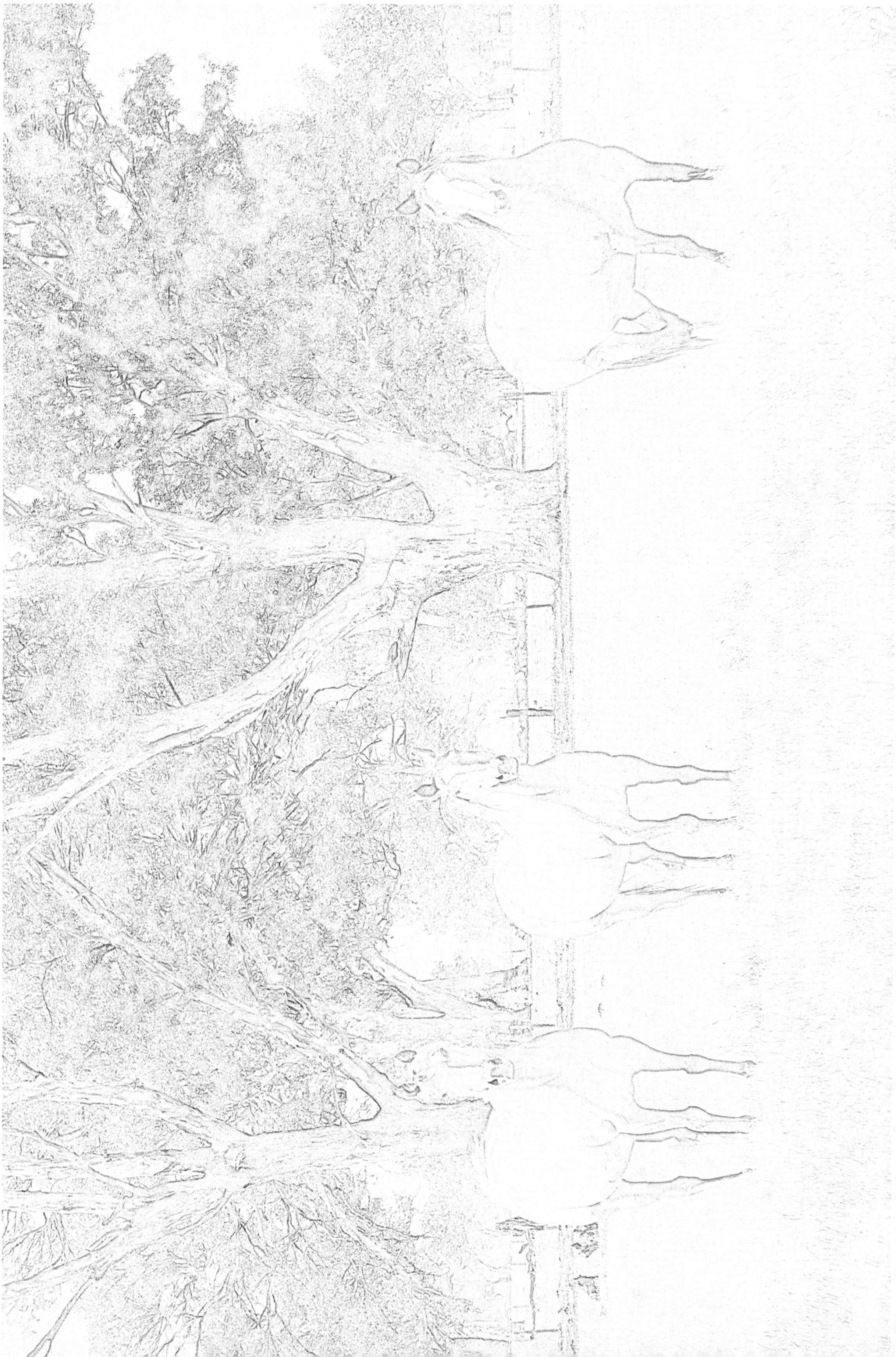

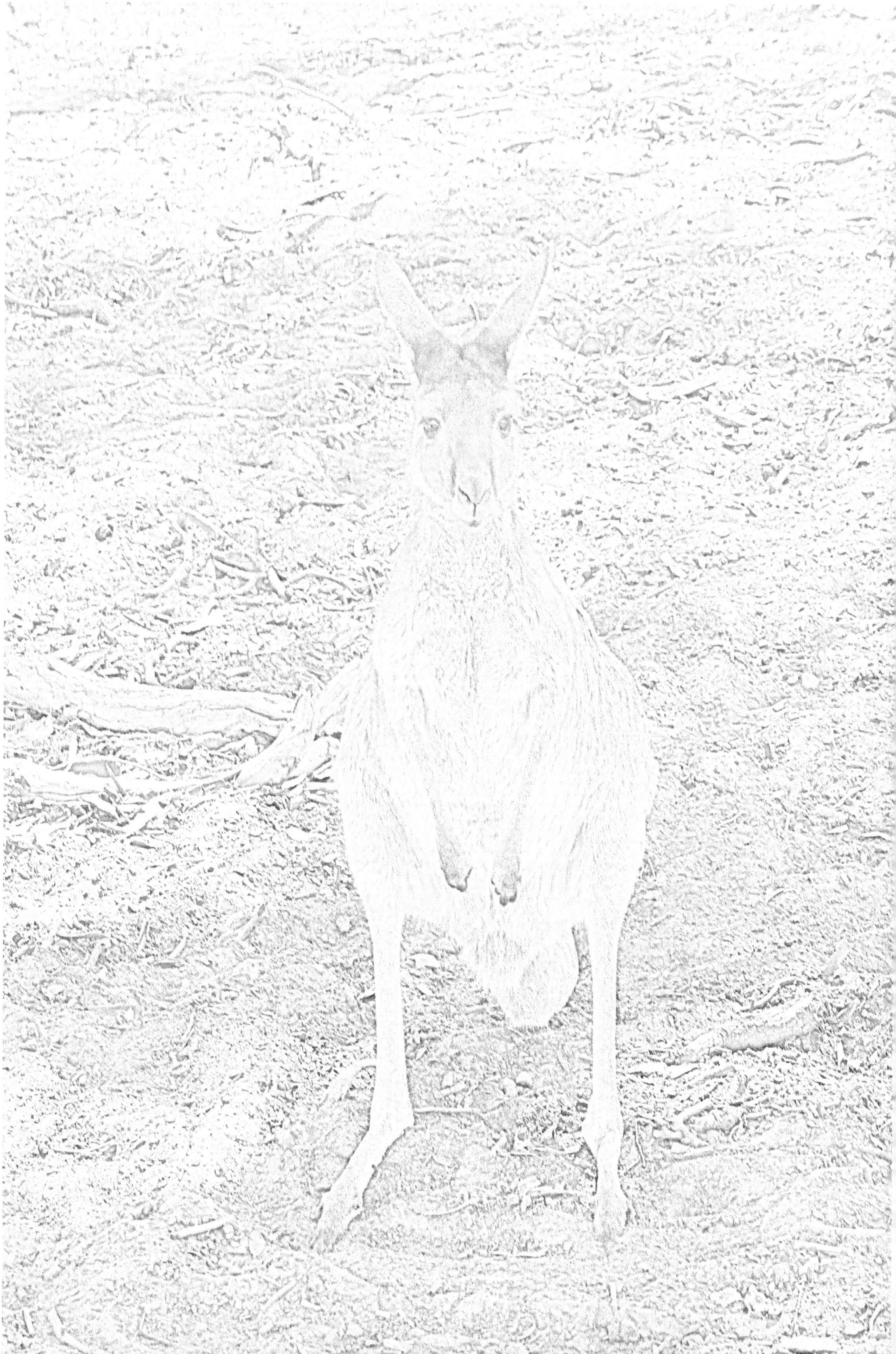

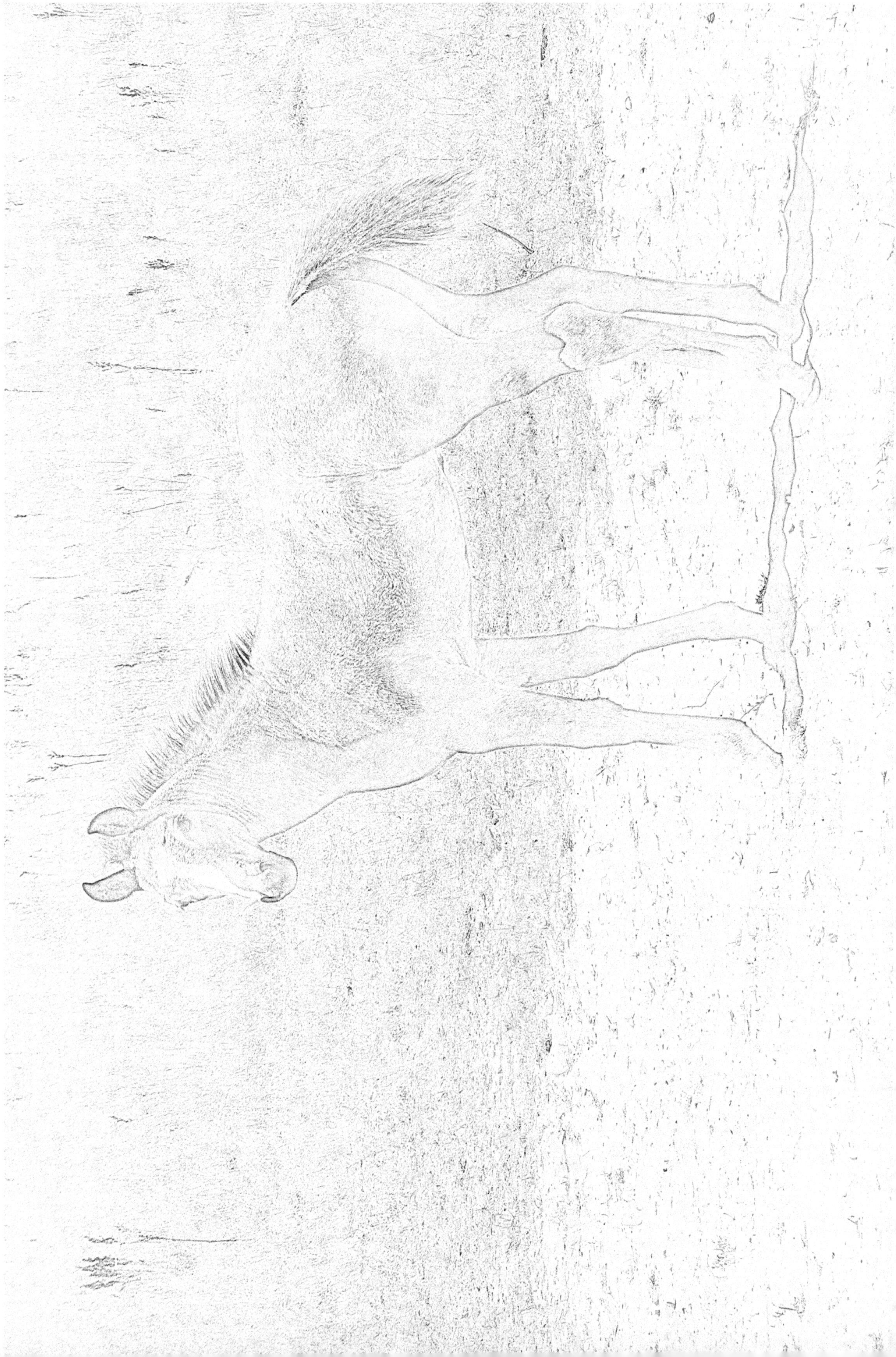

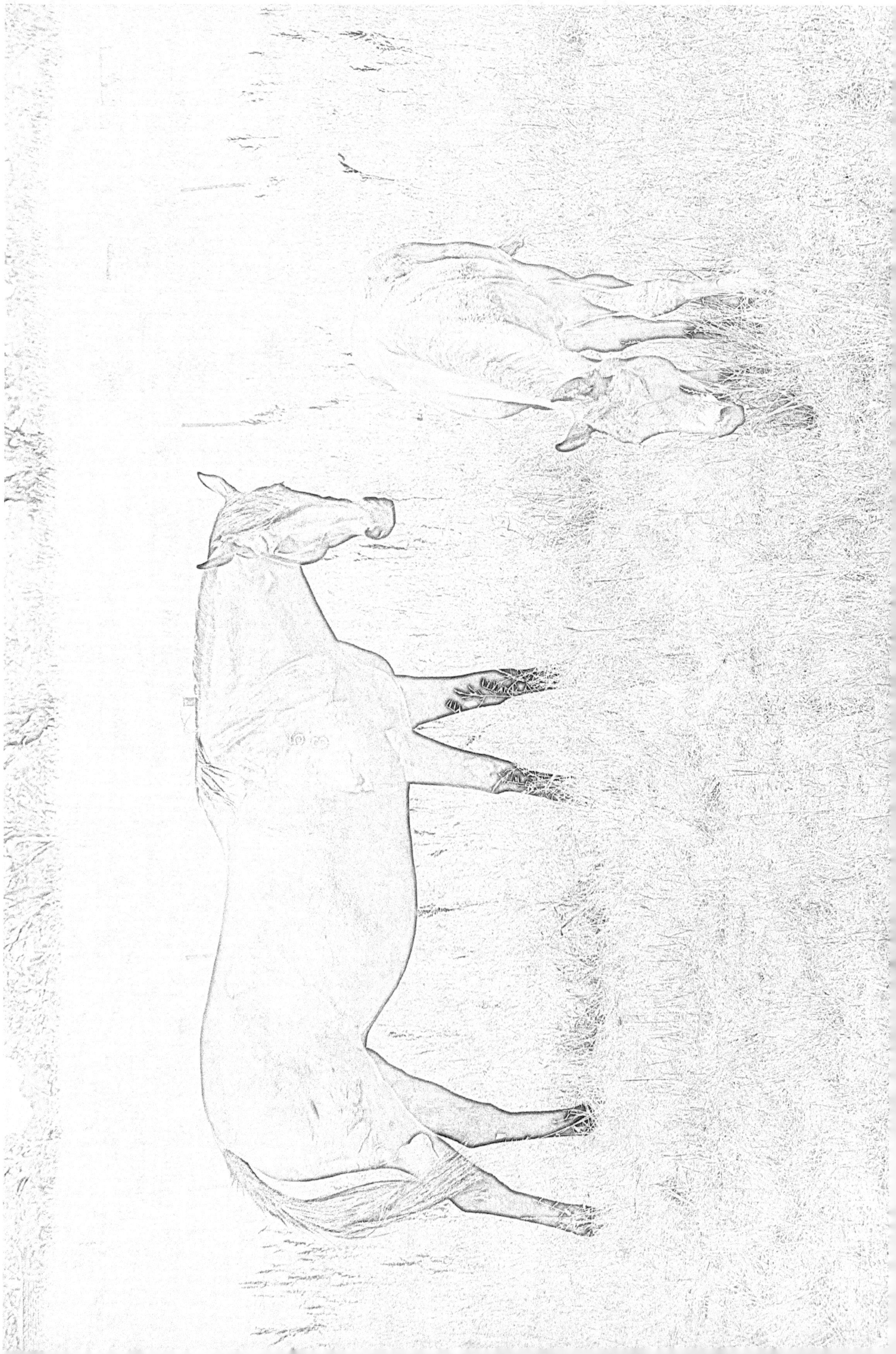

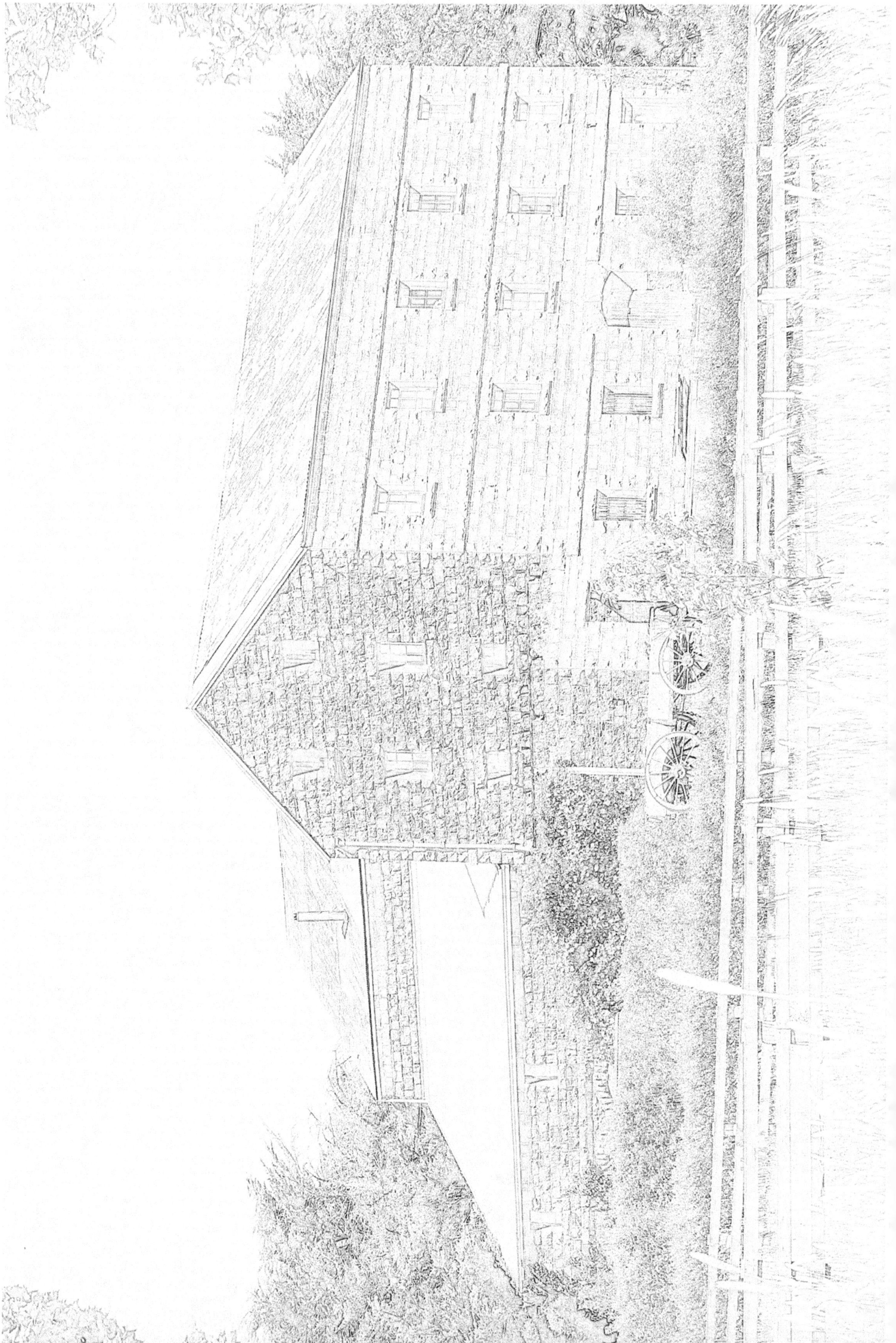

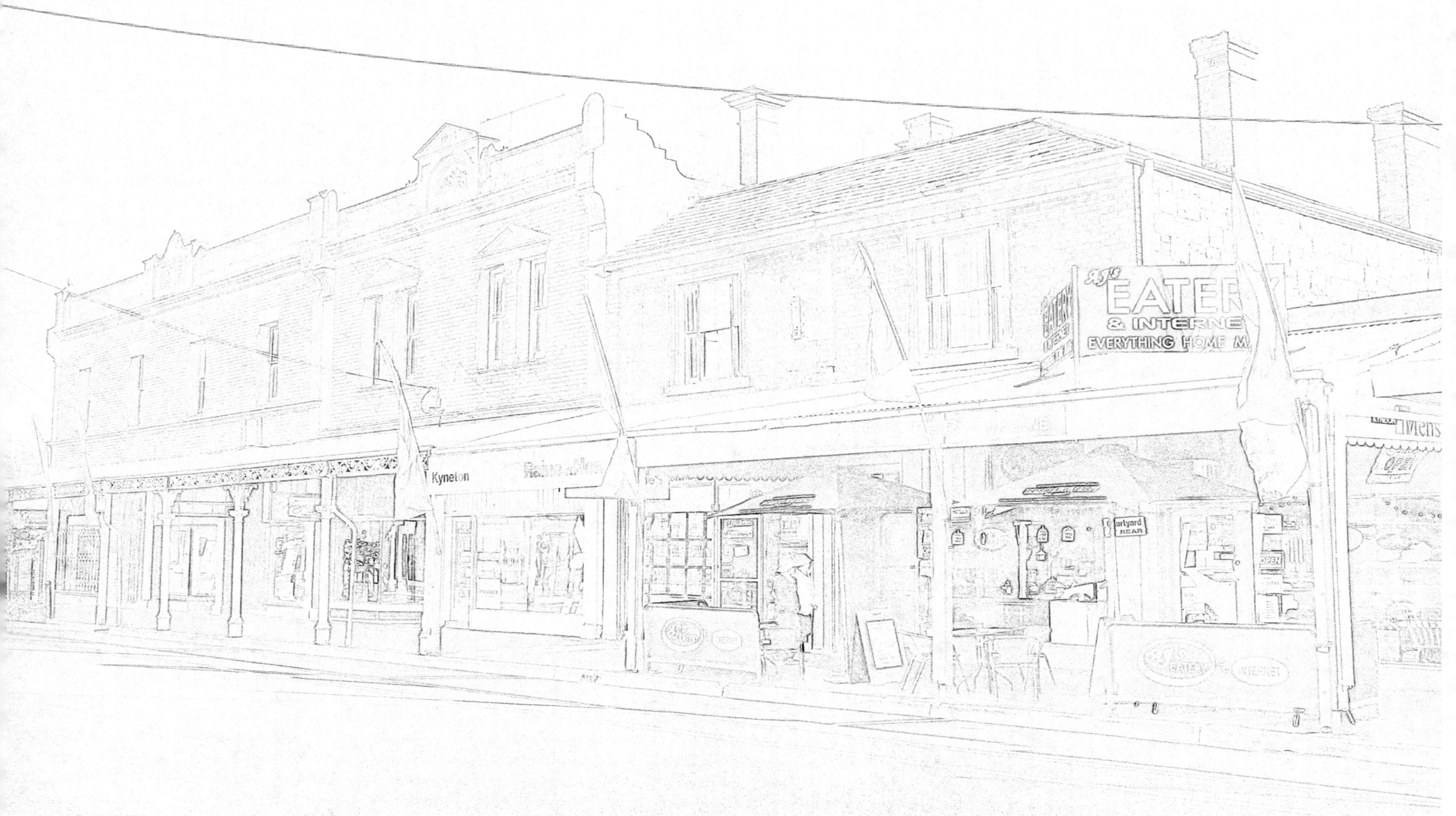
RJ's
EATER
& INTERNE
EVERYTHING HOME M
Kyneton
OPEN
INTERNET

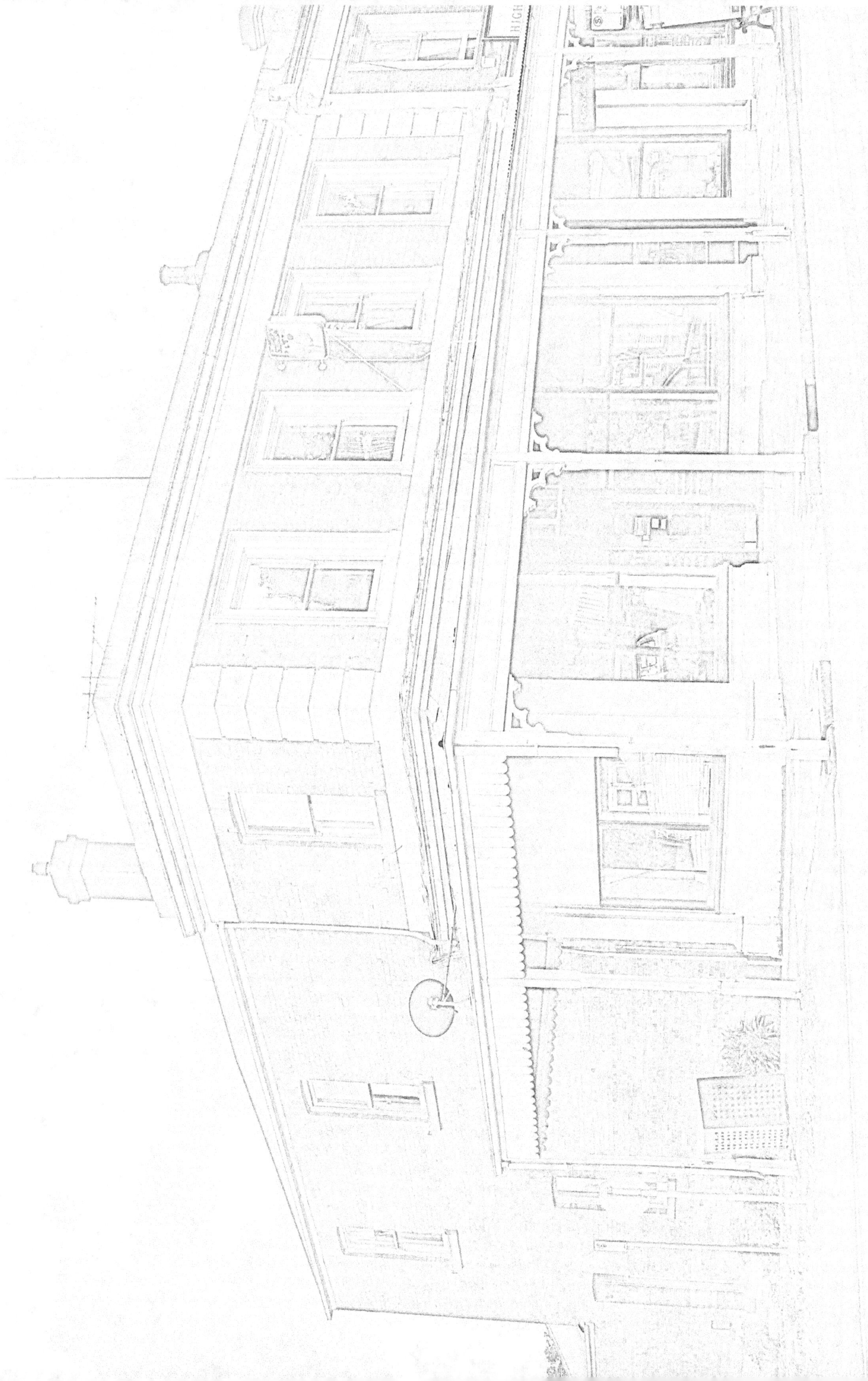

POST
KYNETON POST OFFICE
WHEN FLASHING GIVE WAY TO PEDS

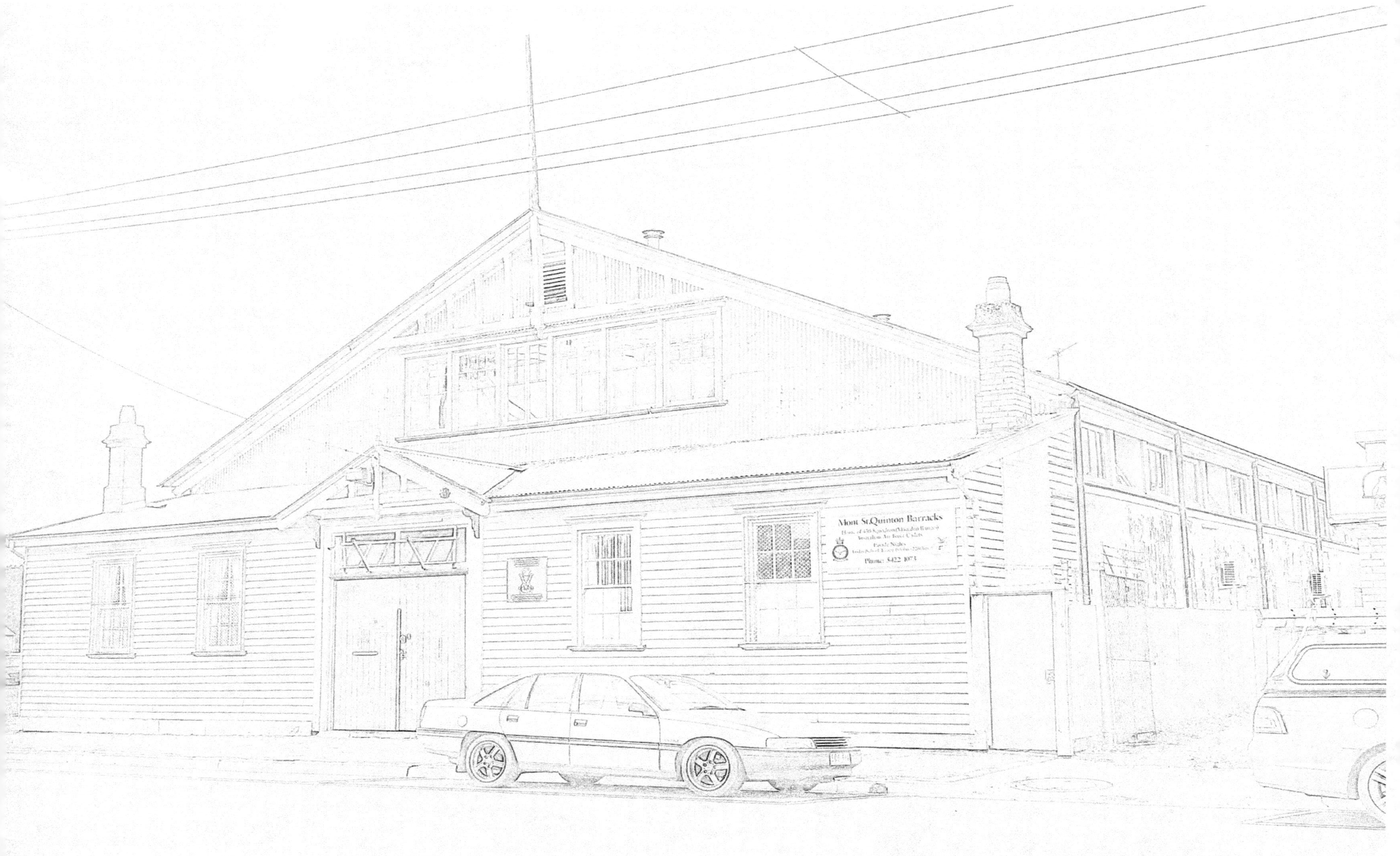
Mont St.Quinton Barracks
Phone: 5422 1073

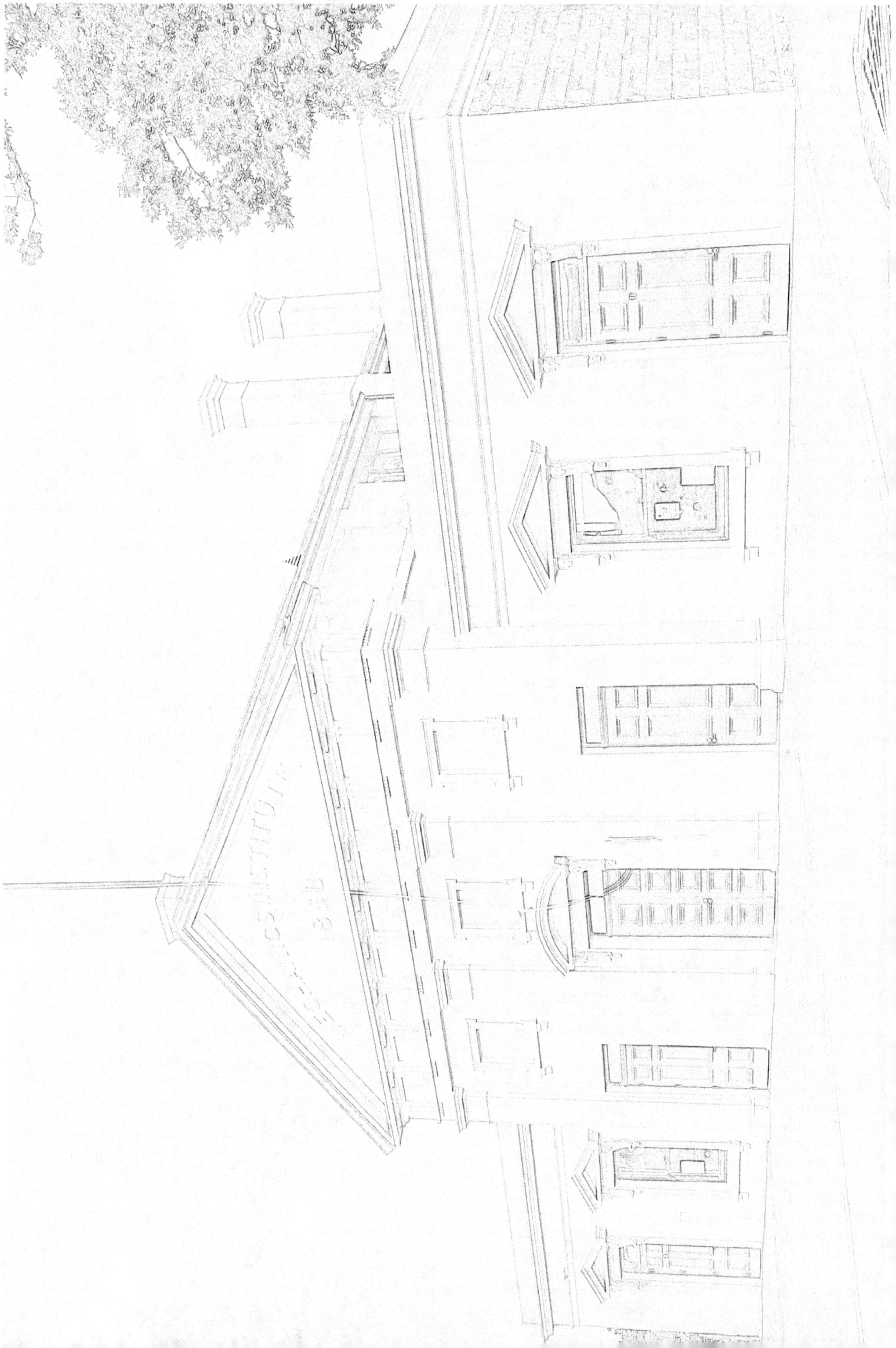

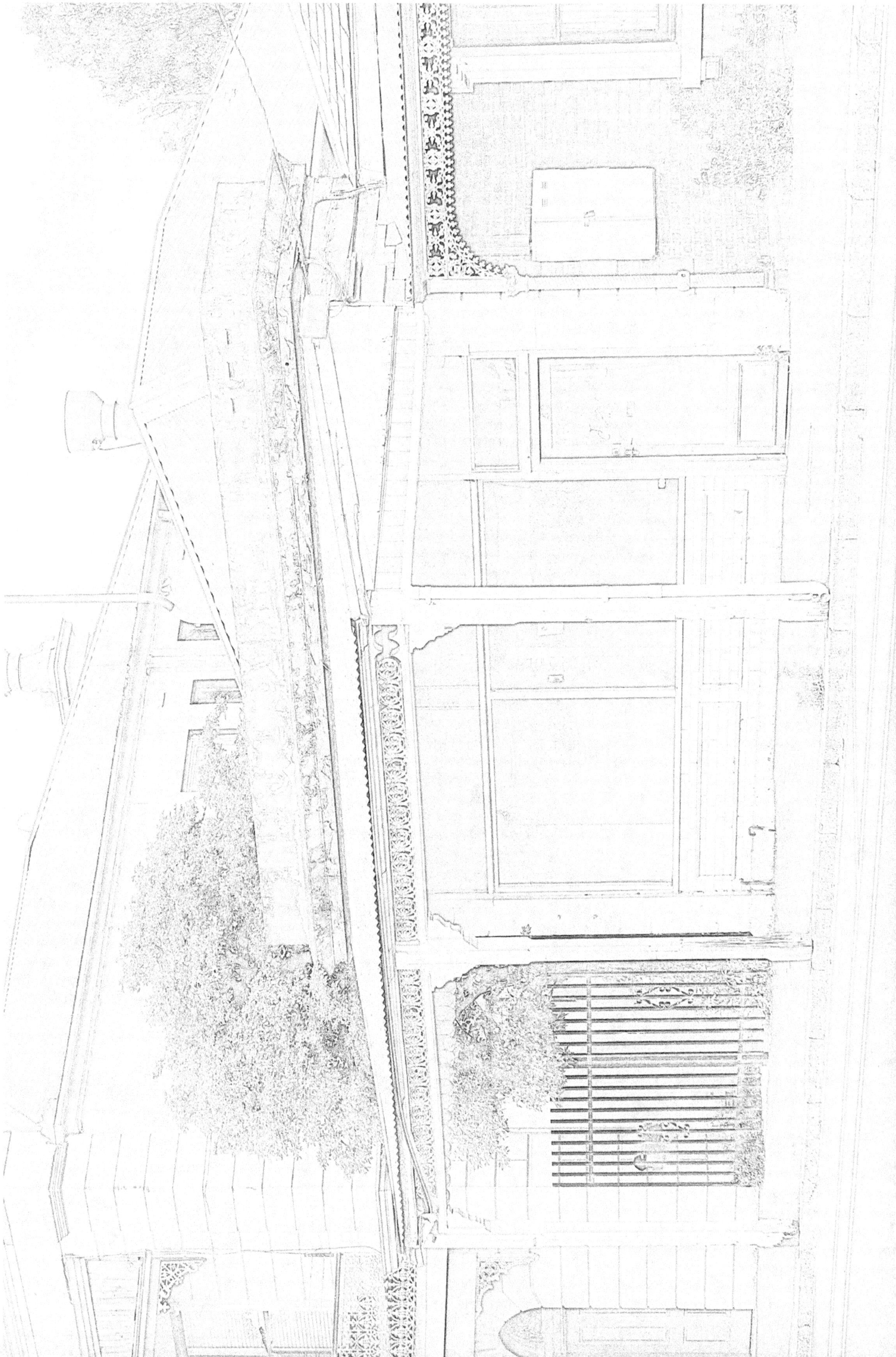

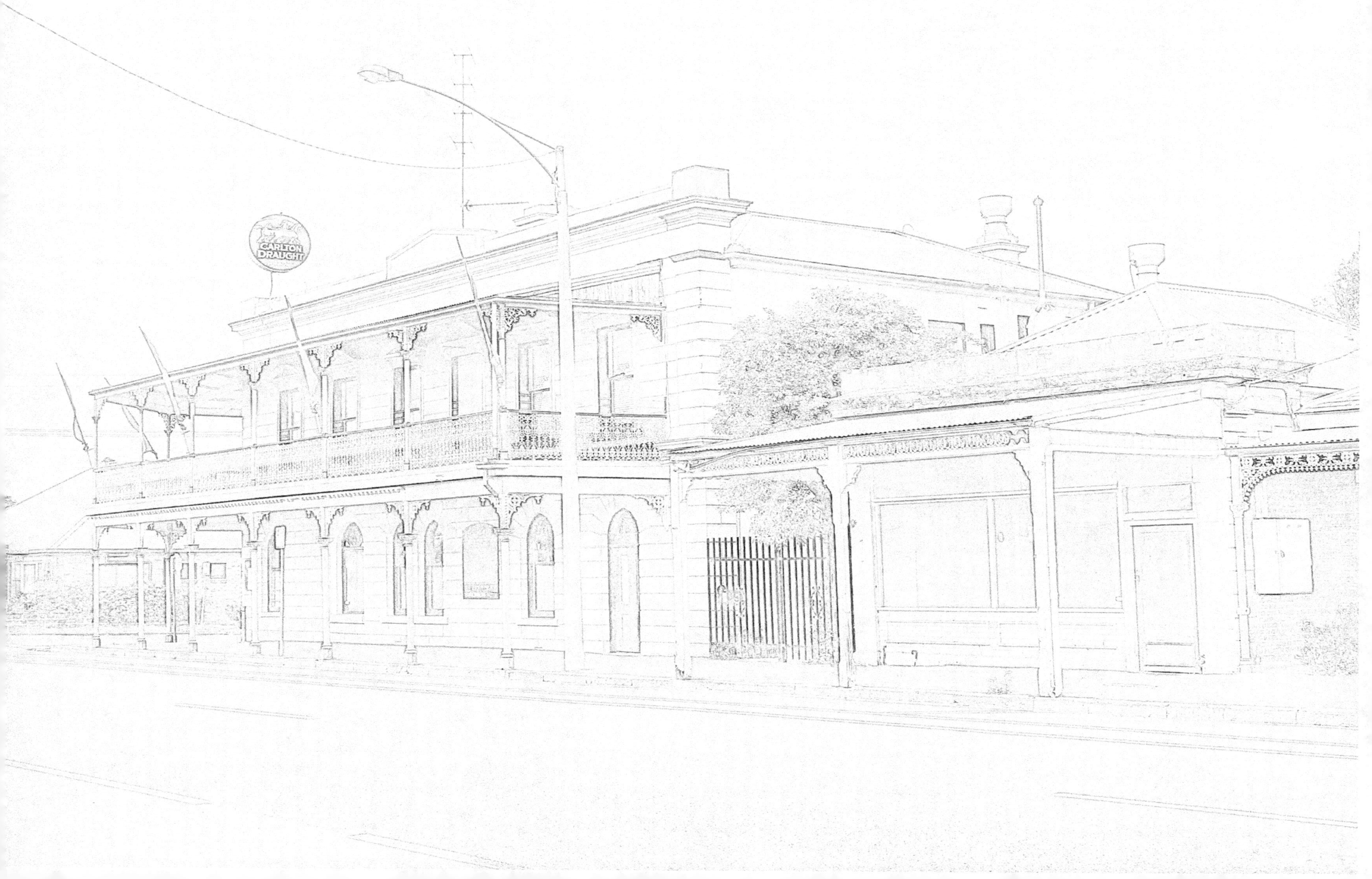
CARLTON DRAUGHT

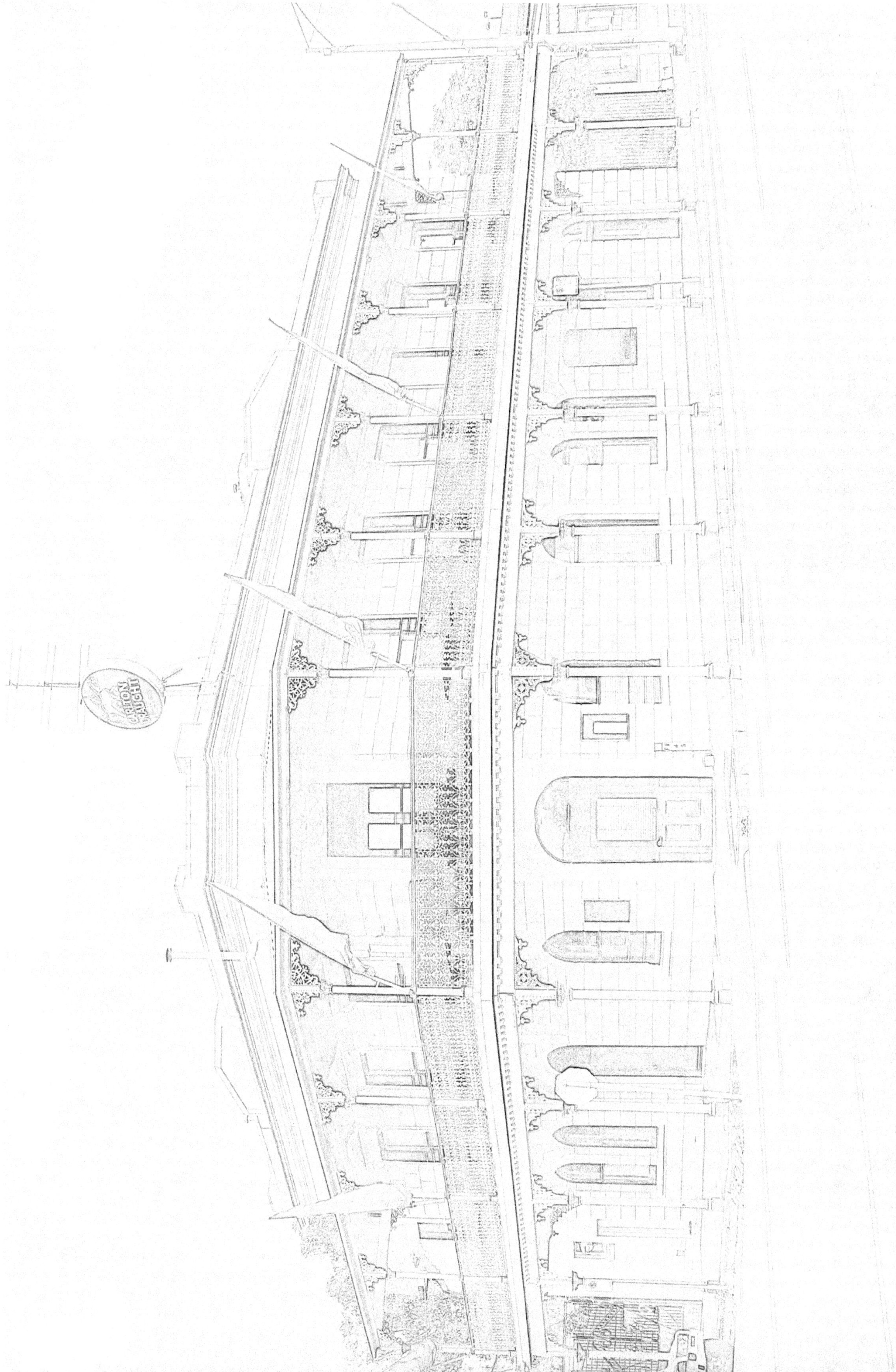
CARLTON DRAUGHT

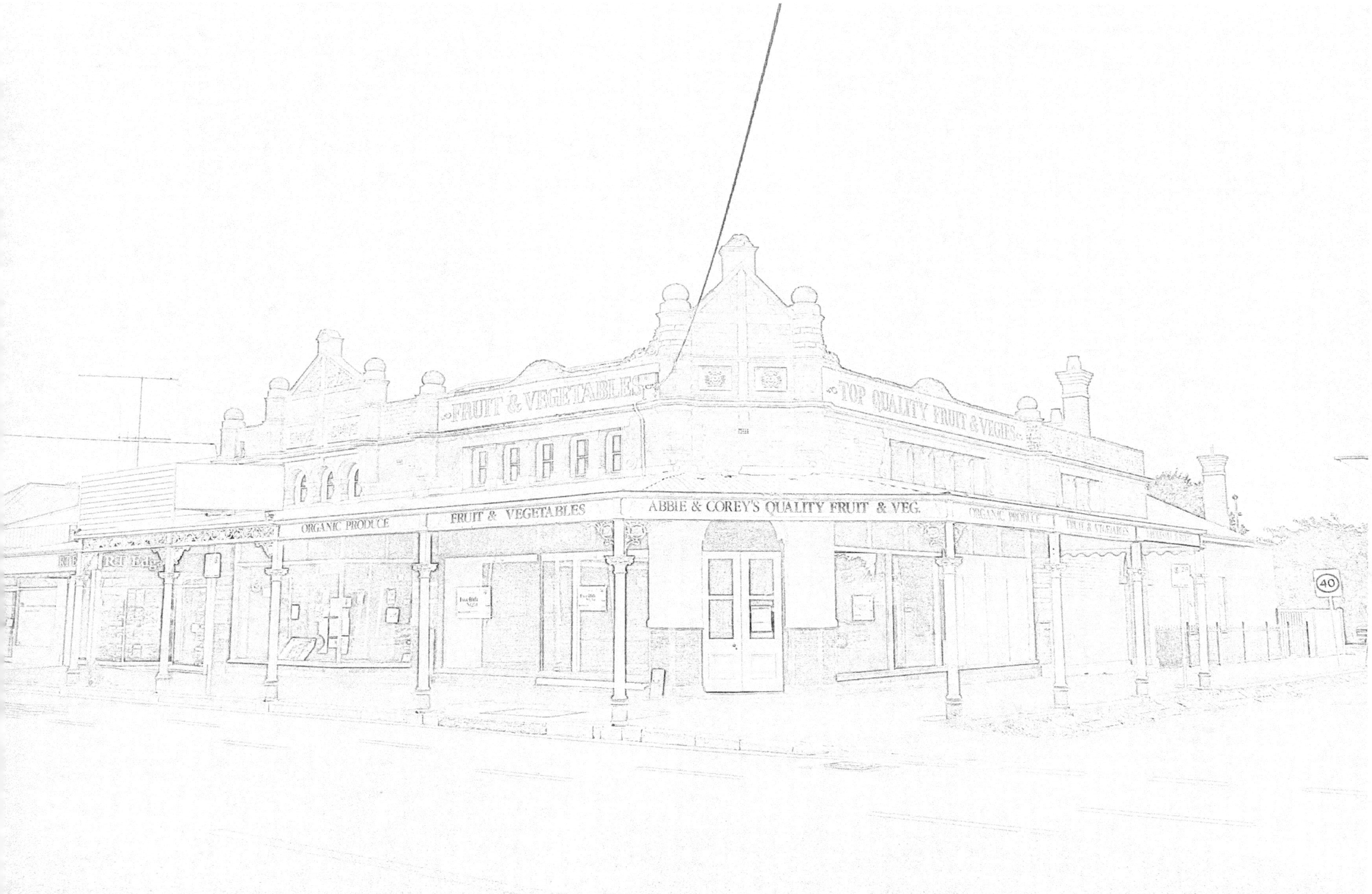

FRUIT & VEGETABLES
TOP QUALITY FRUIT & VEGIES
ORGANIC PRODUCE
FRUIT & VEGETABLES
ABBIE & COREY'S QUALITY FRUIT & VEG.
ORGANIC PRODUCE
FRUIT & VEGETABLES
40

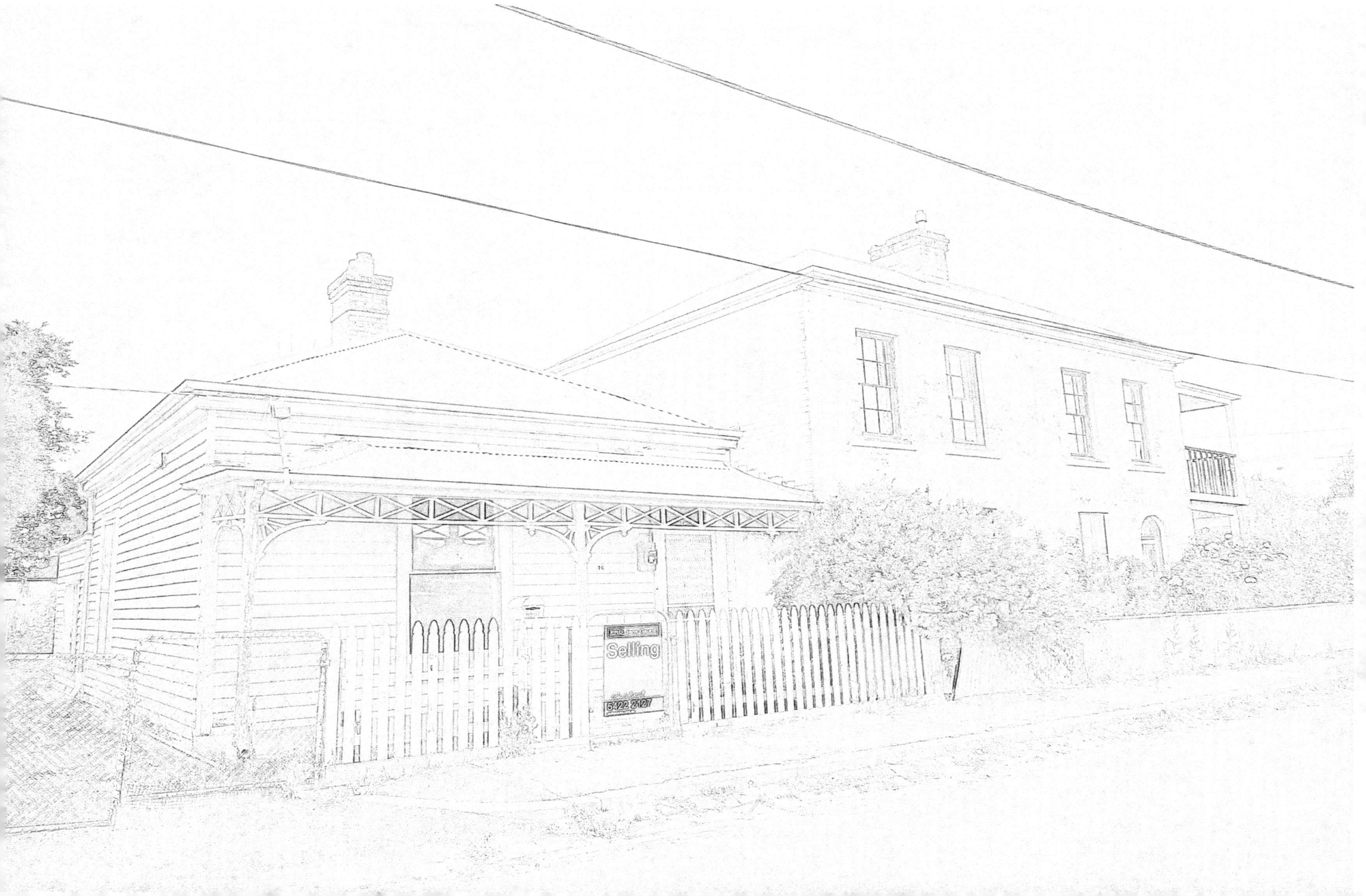
Selling
5422 2127

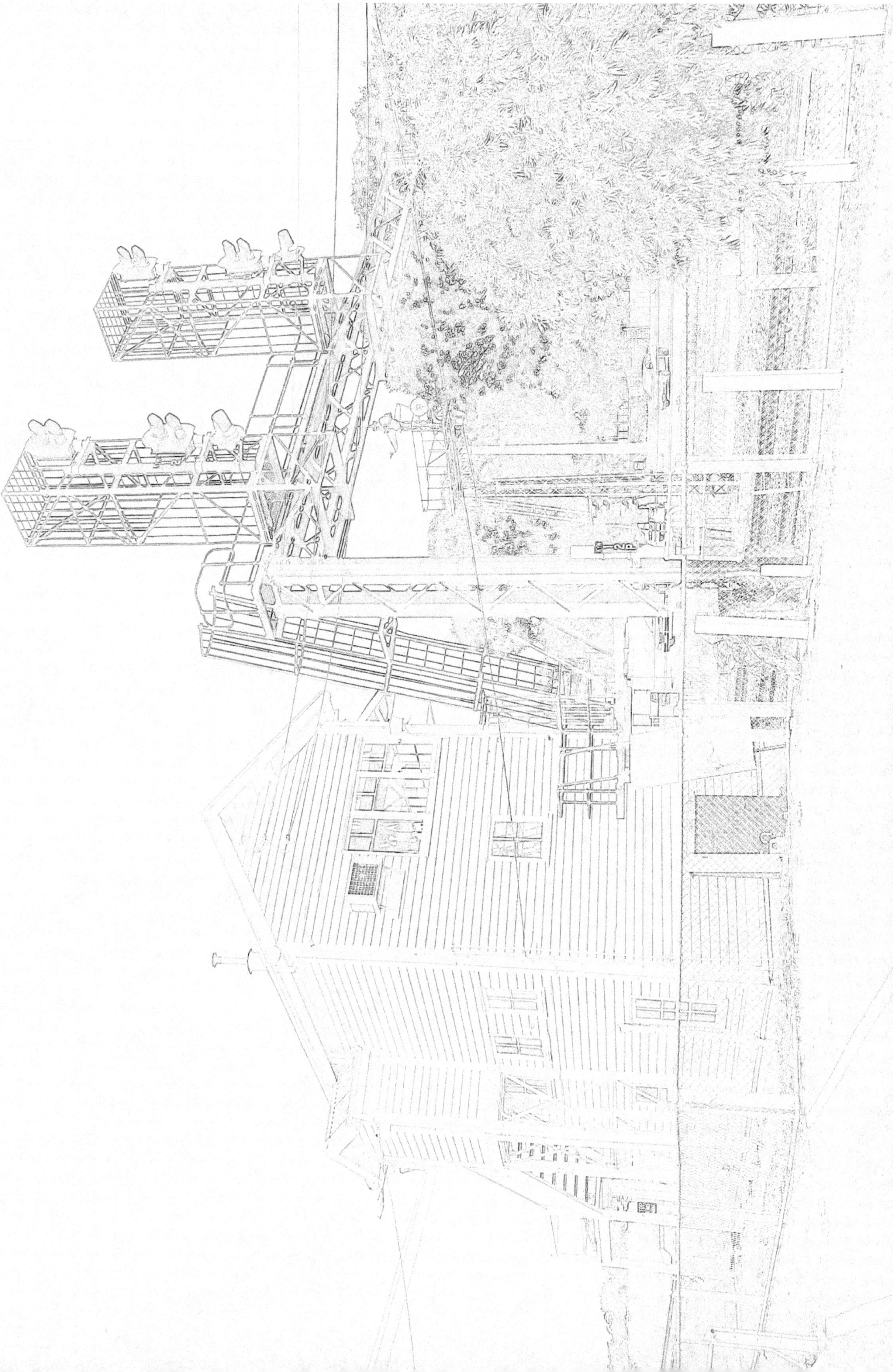

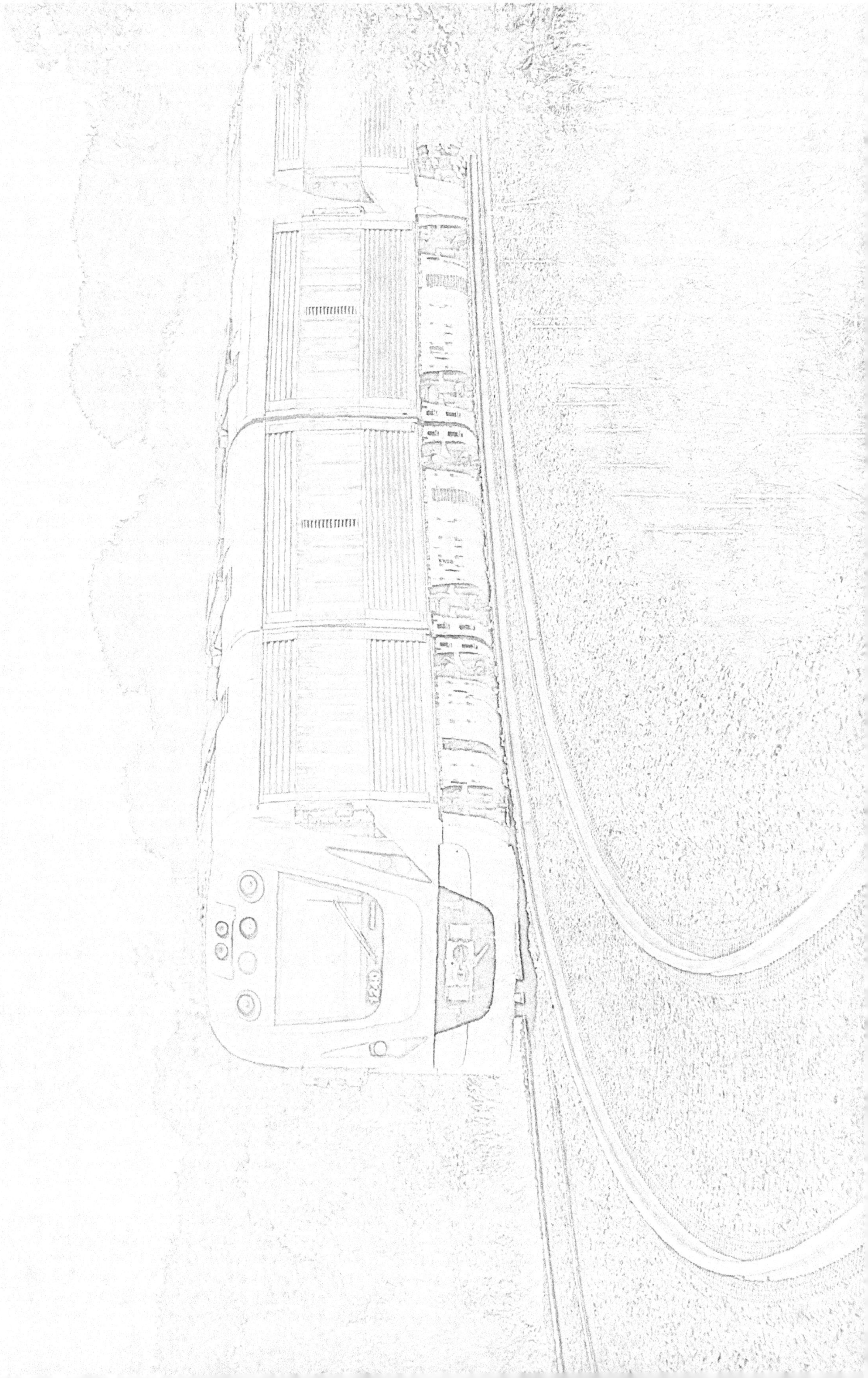

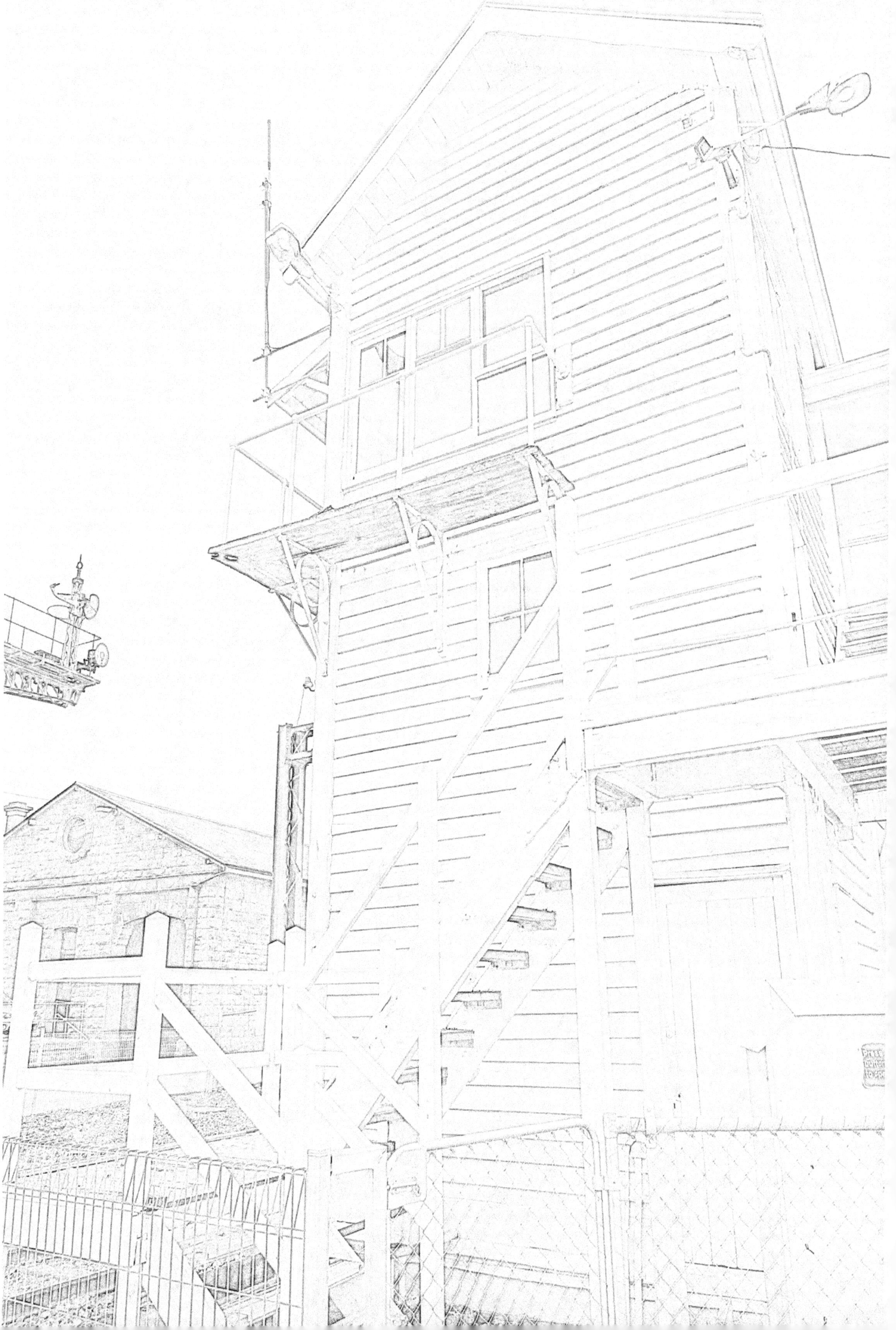

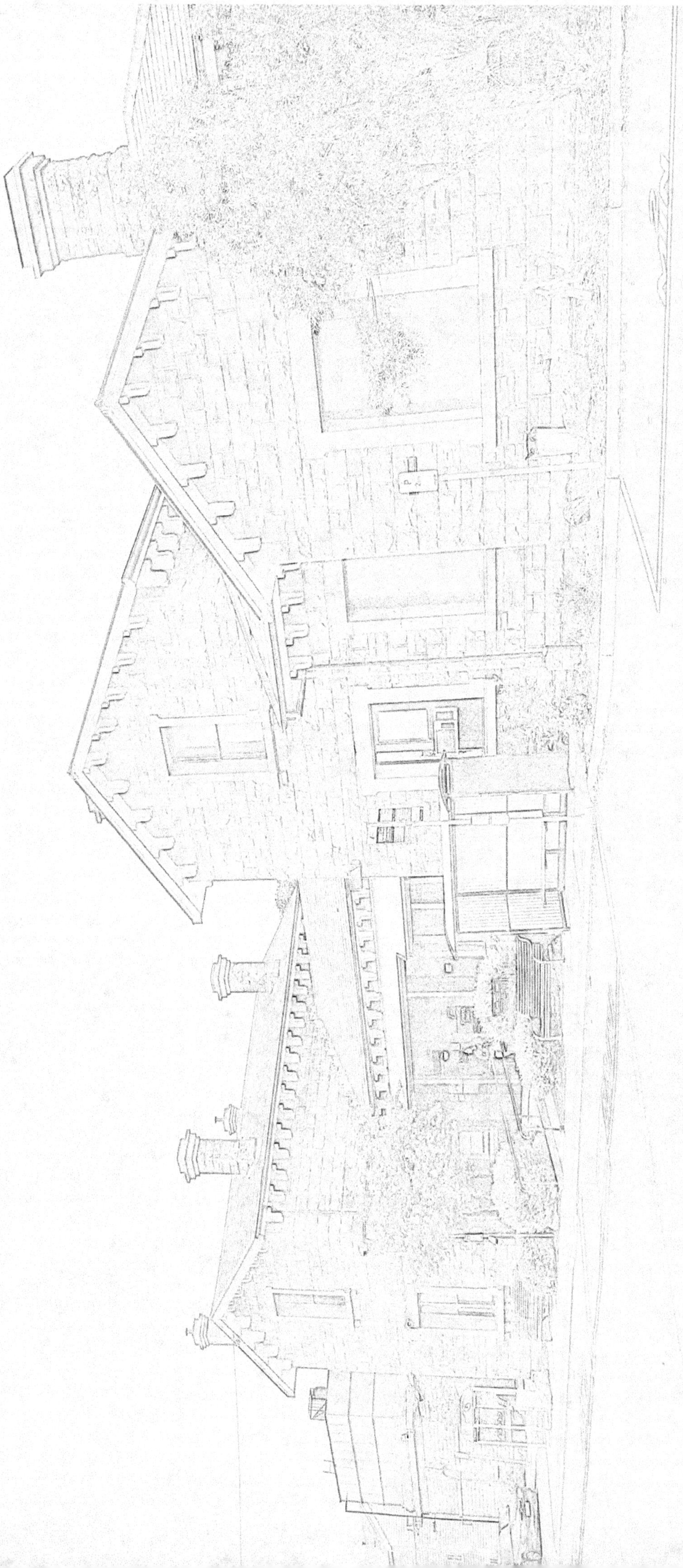

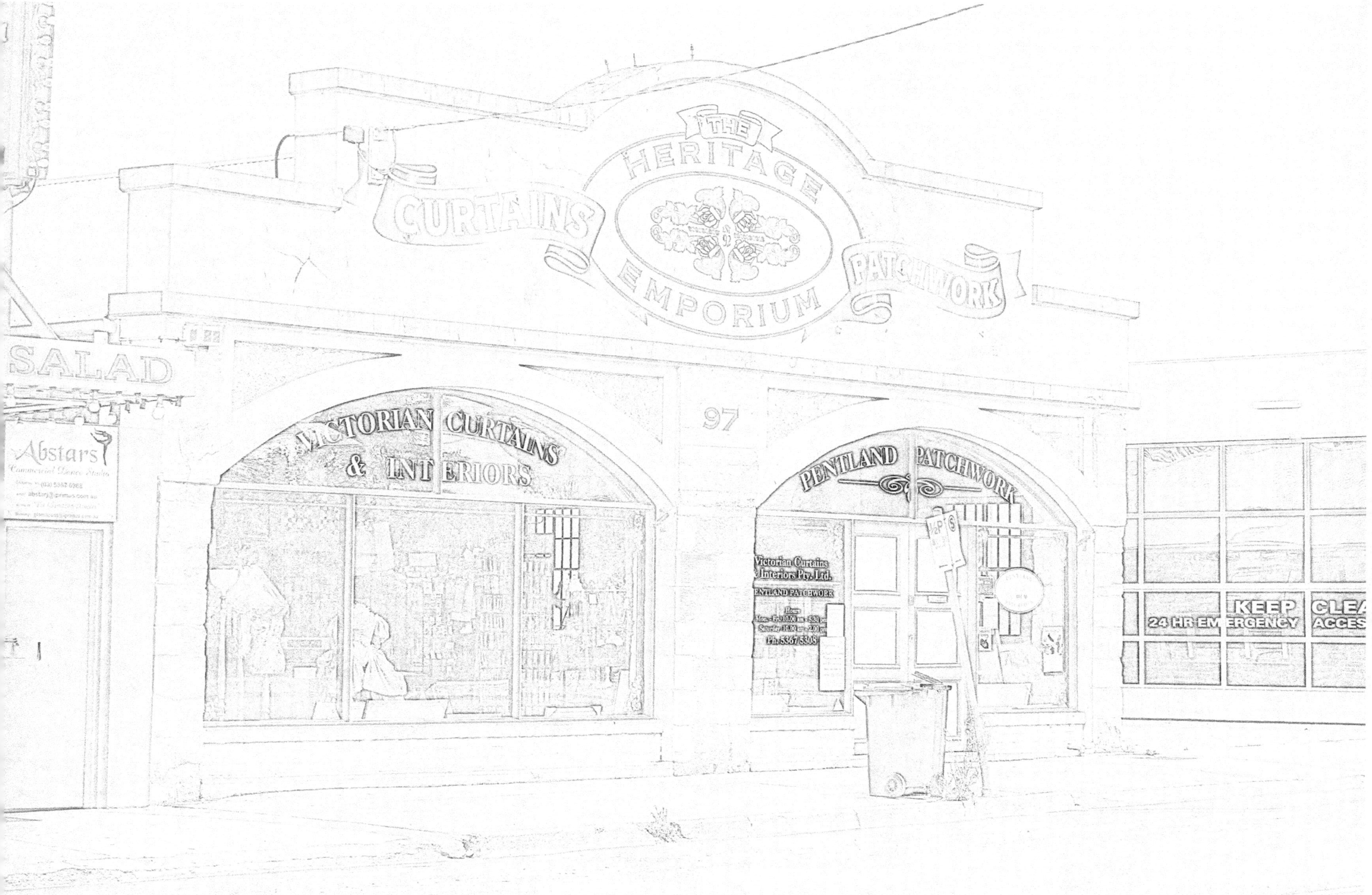
THE
HERITAGE
CURTAINS
EMPORIUM
PATCHWORK
SALAD
Abstars
97
VICTORIAN CURTAINS
& INTERIORS
PENTLAND PATCHWORK
Victorian Curtains
& Interiors Pty. Ltd.
PENTLAND PATCHWORK
Ph. 5367 5308
KEEP CLEA
24 HR EMERGENCY ACCES

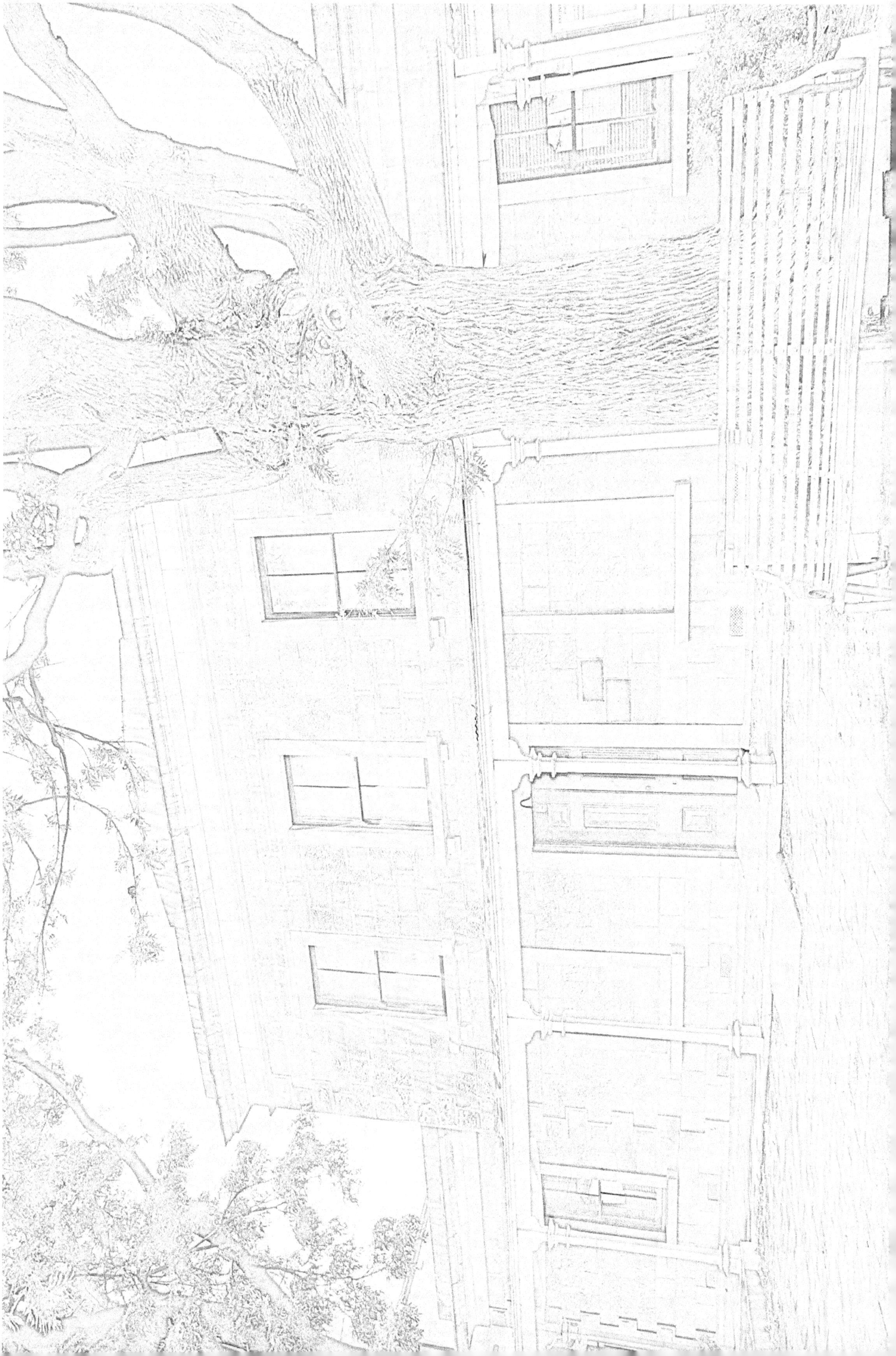

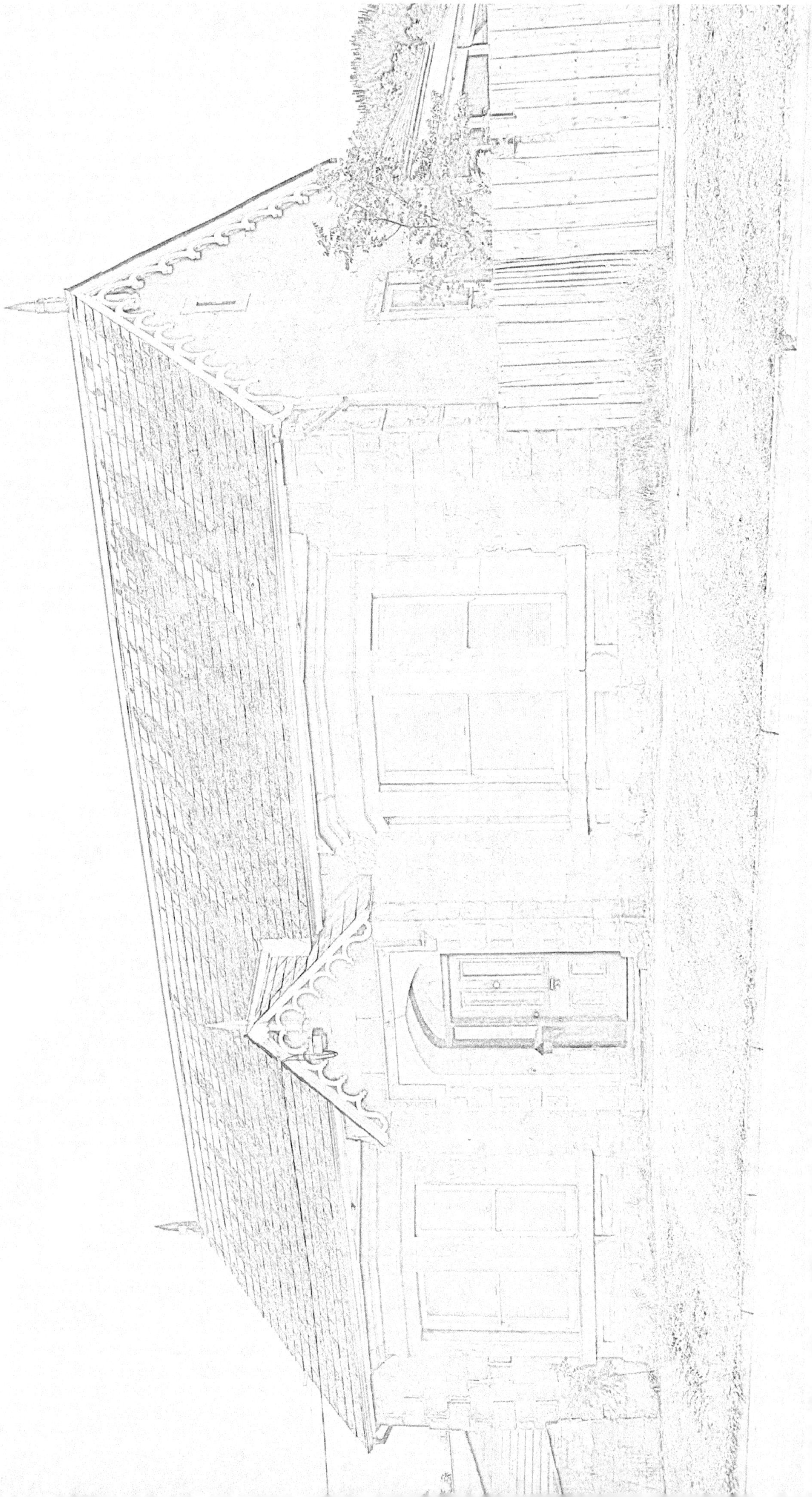

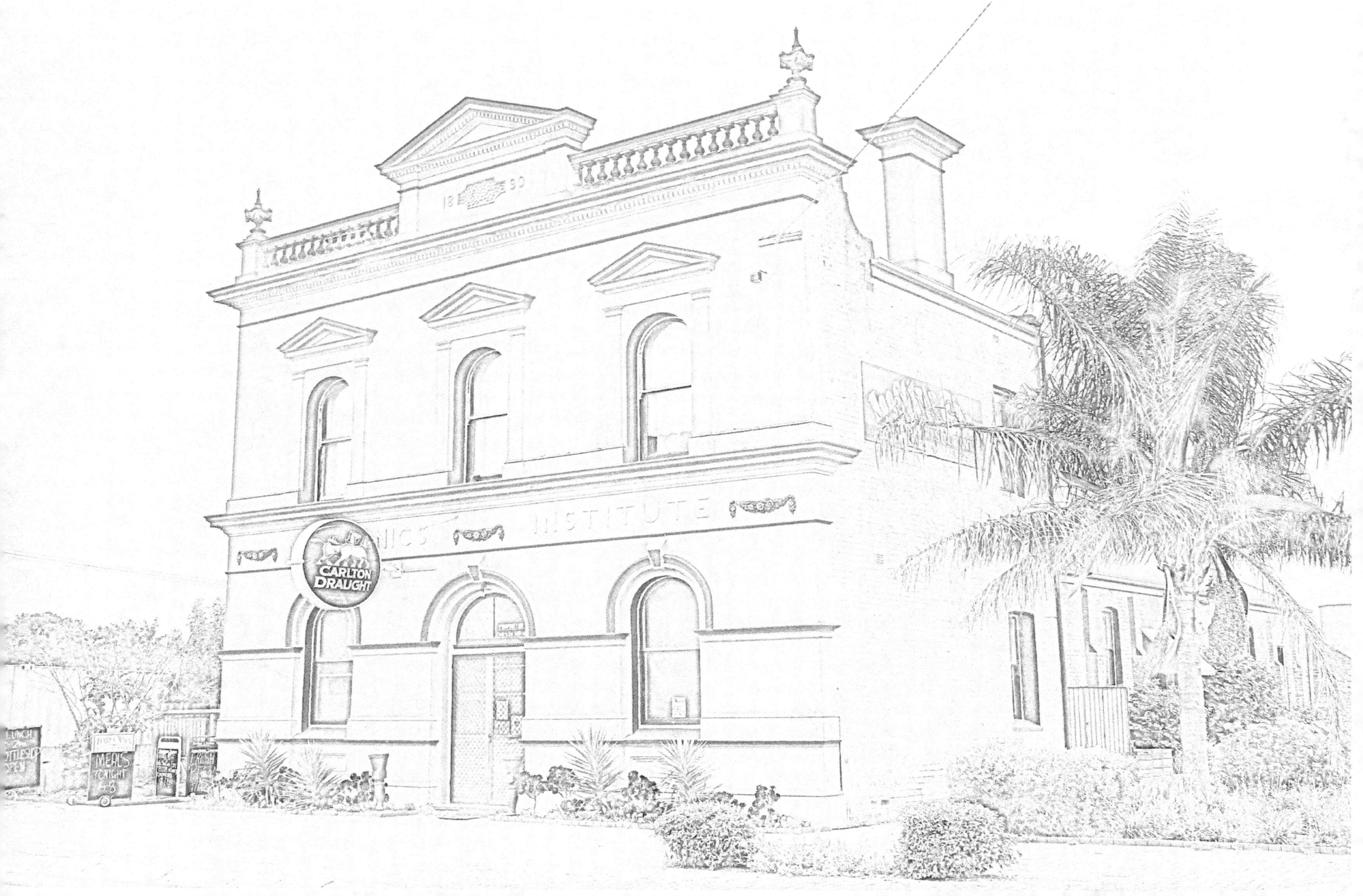
18 90
INSTITUTE
CARLTON DRAUGHT
MEALS TONIGHT

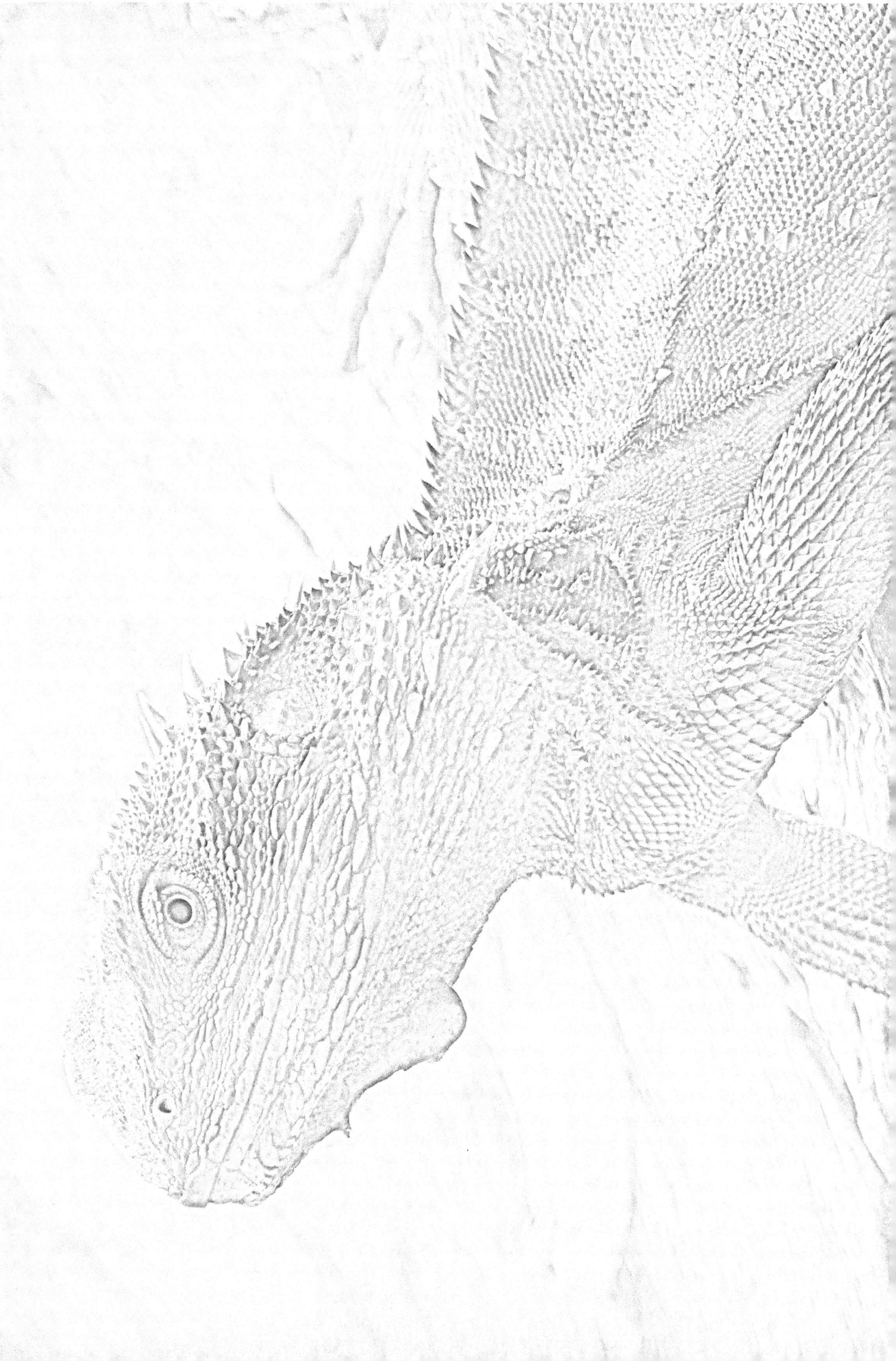

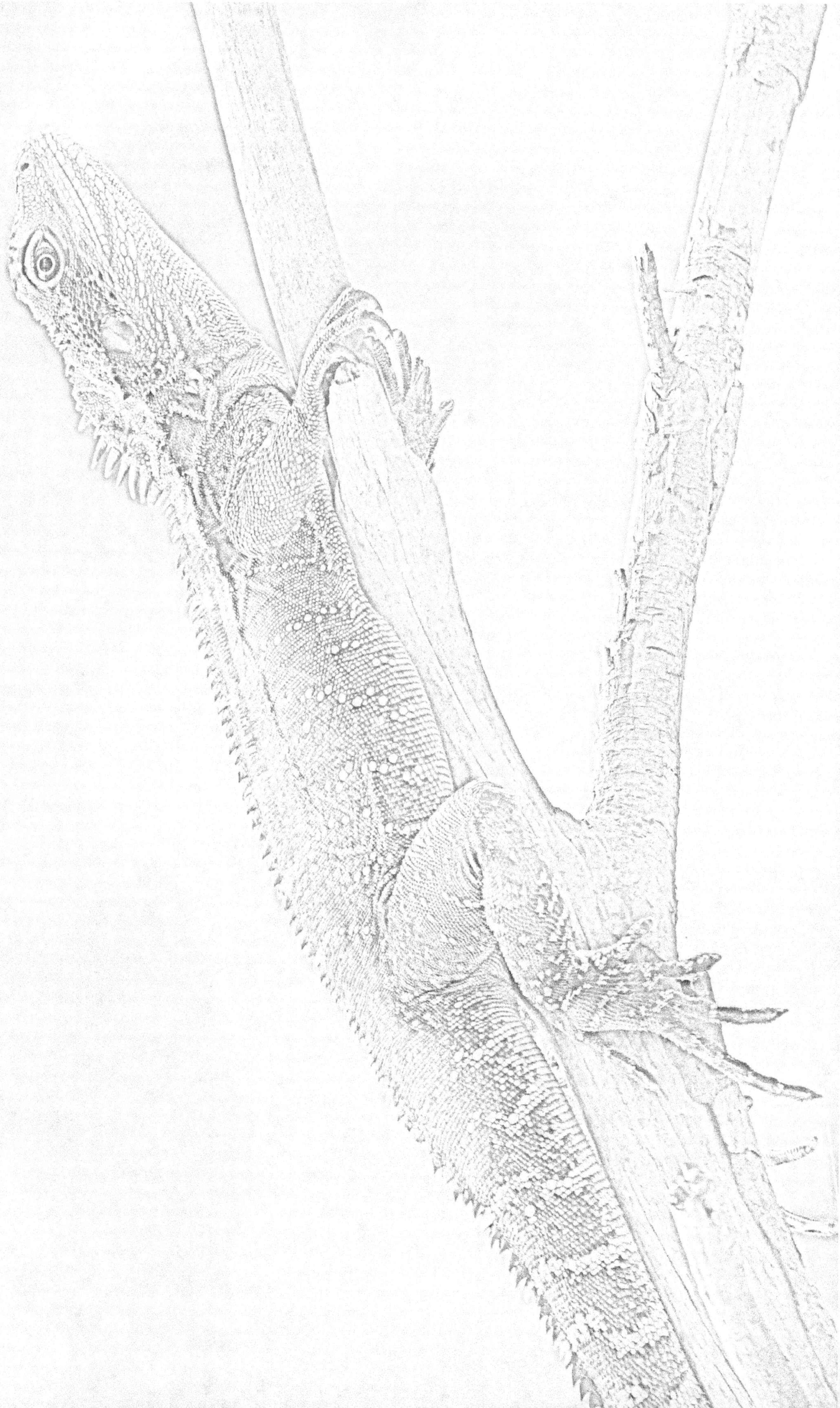

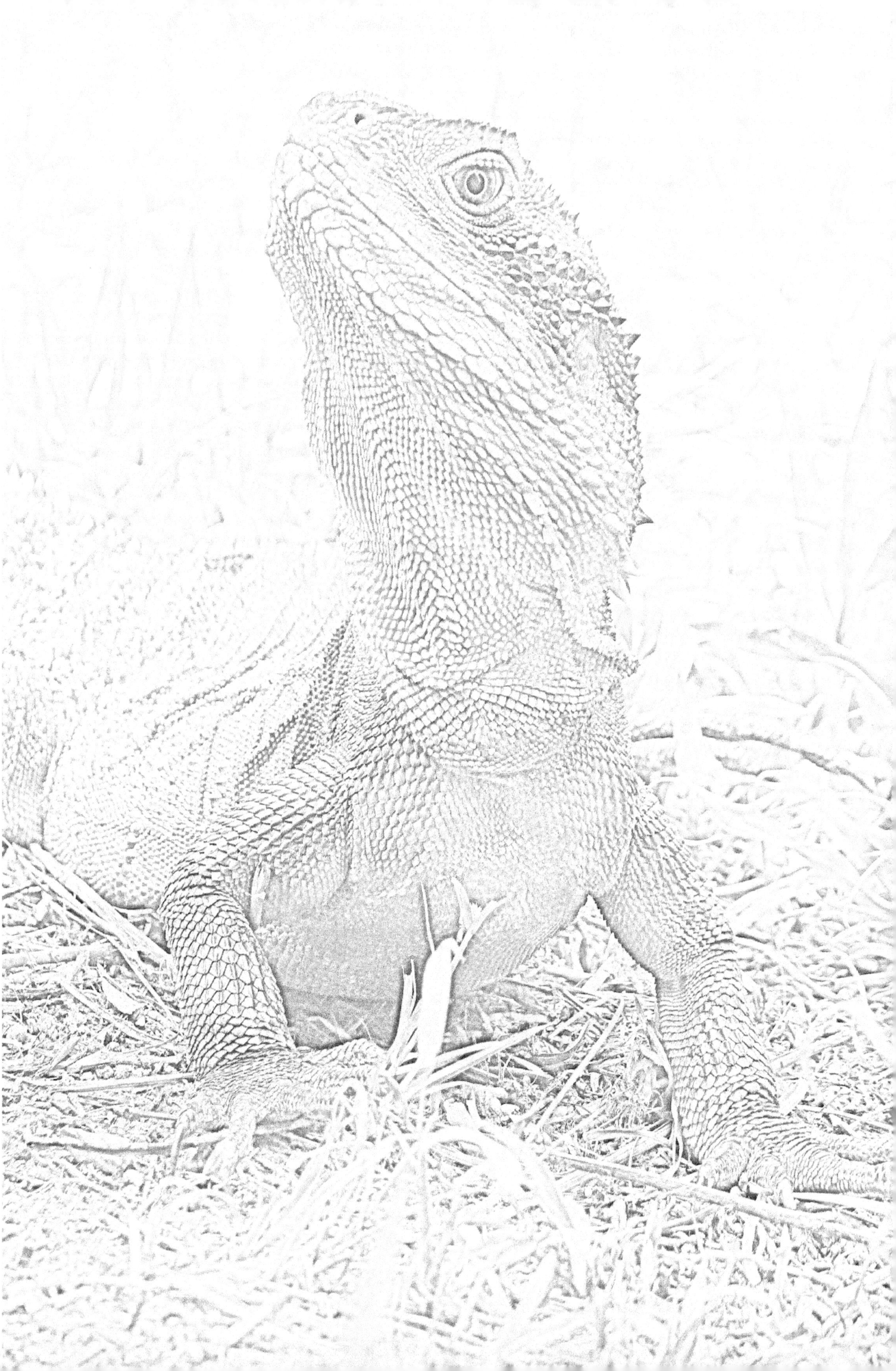

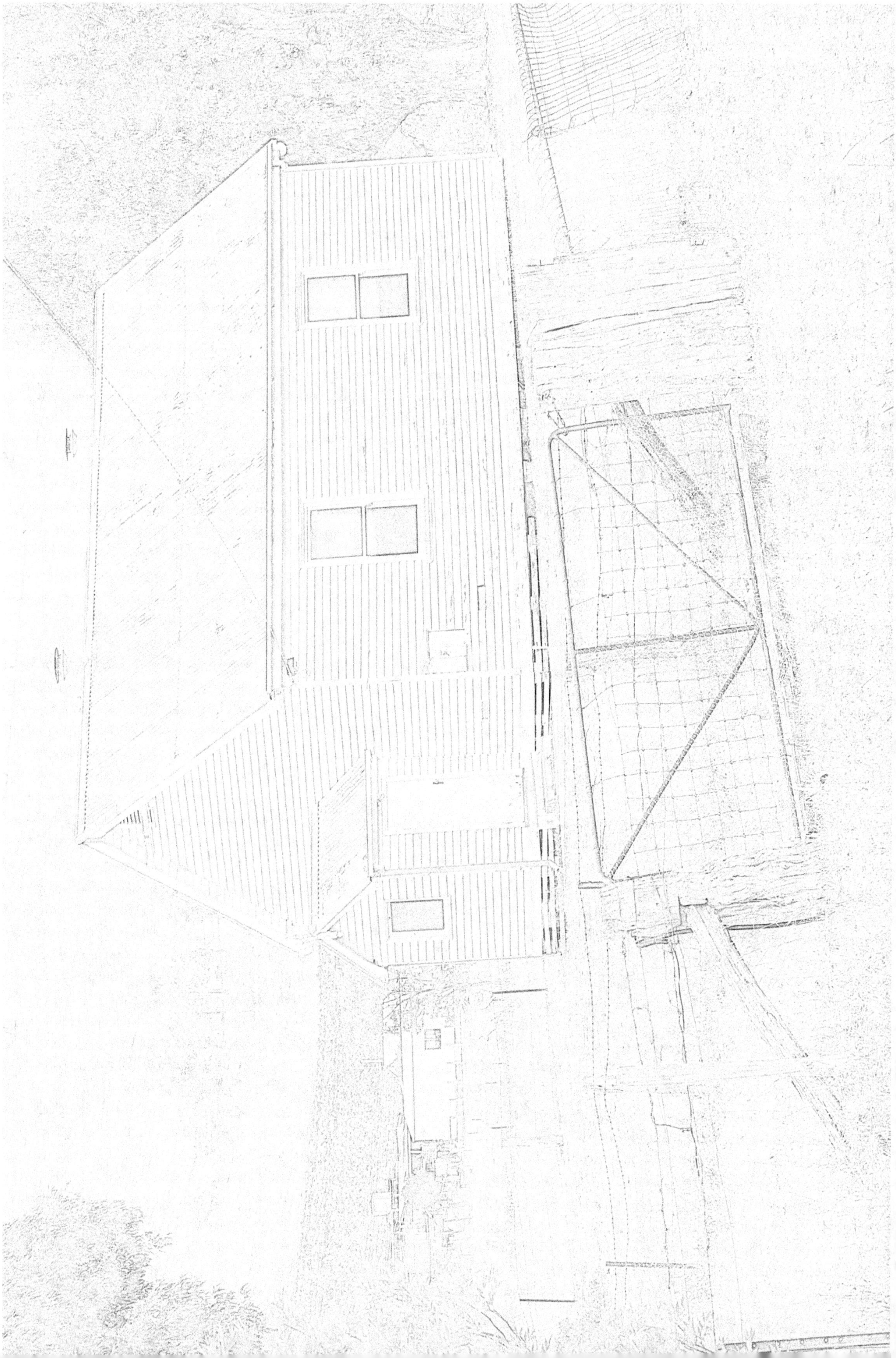

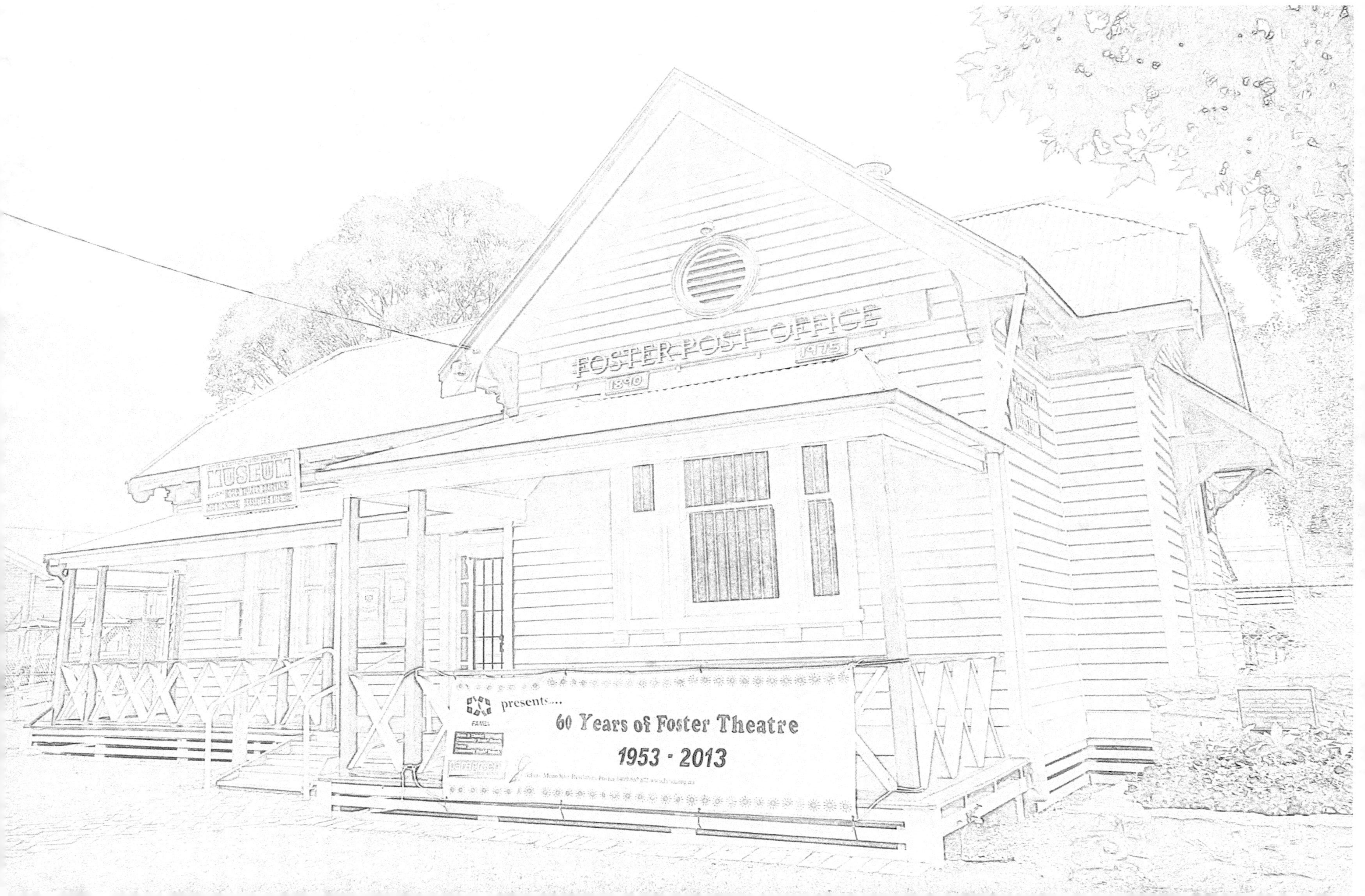

FOSTER POST OFFICE
1890
1975
MUSEUM
presents....
60 Years of Foster Theatre
1953 - 2013

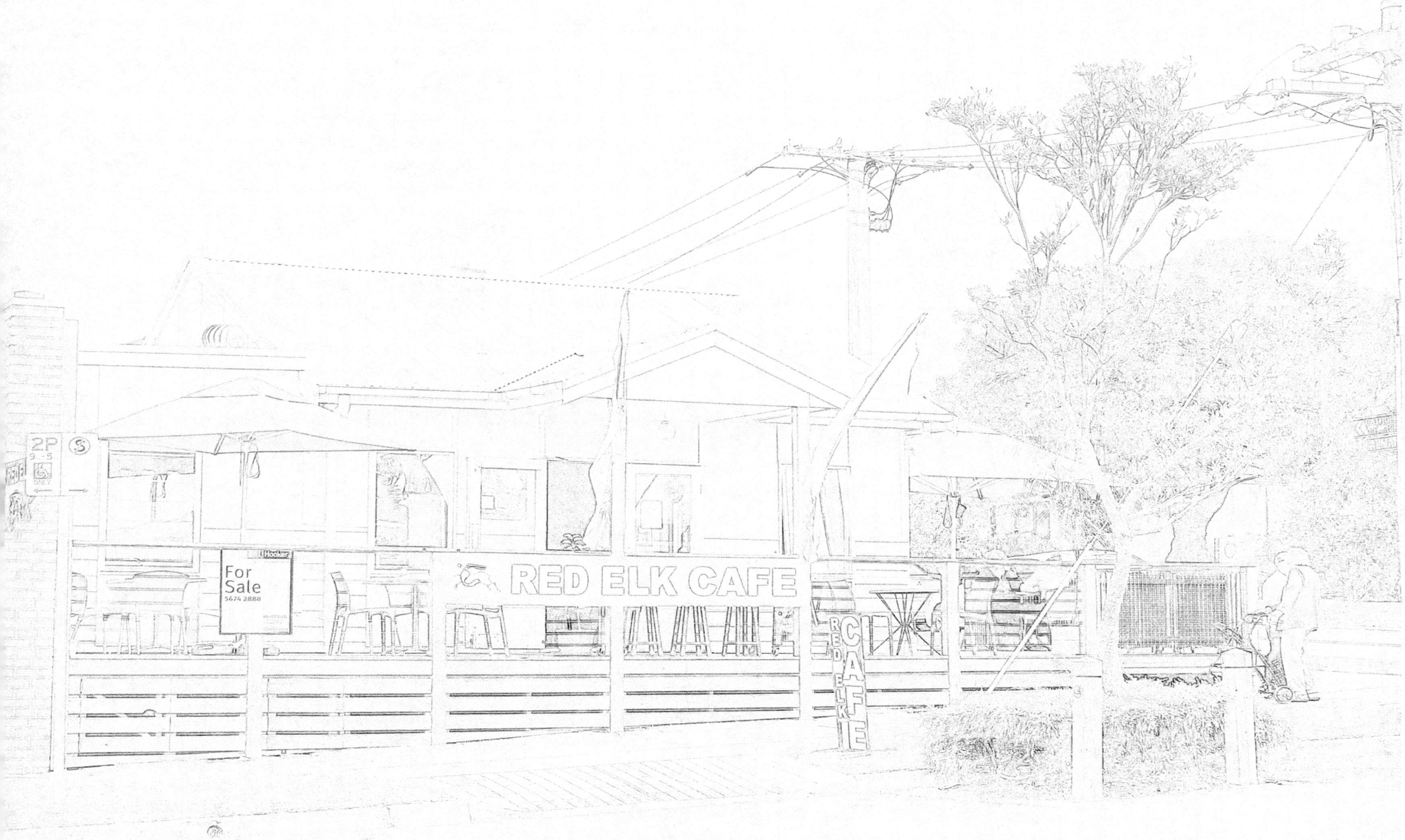
2P
For Sale
5674 2888
RED ELK CAFE
RED ELK
CAFE

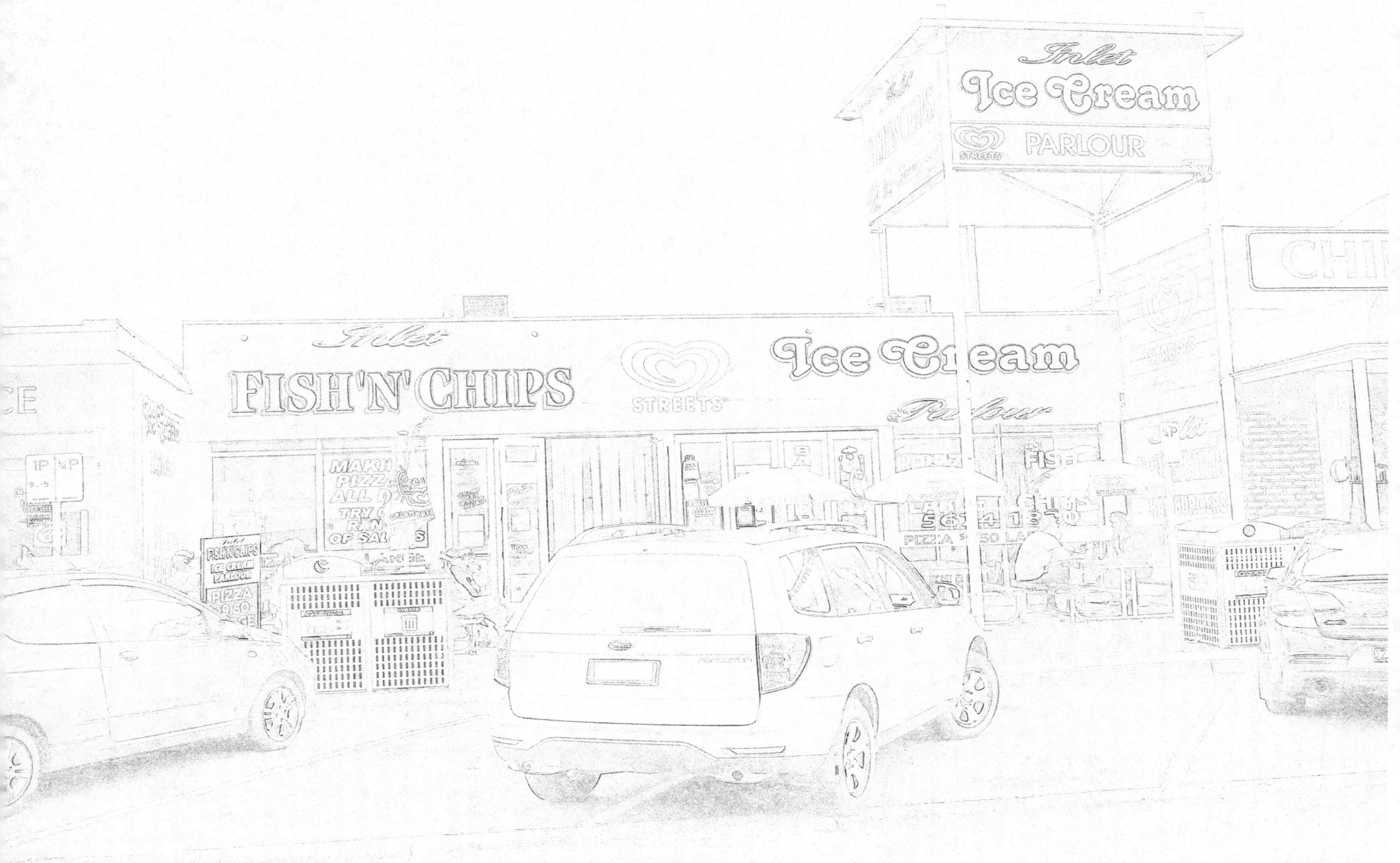
Inlet
Ice Cream
STREETS
PARLOUR
Inlet
FISH'N'CHIPS
STREETS
Ice Cream
Parlour
Inlet
FISH'N'CHIPS
ICE CREAM
PARLOUR
PIZZA
1P
½P

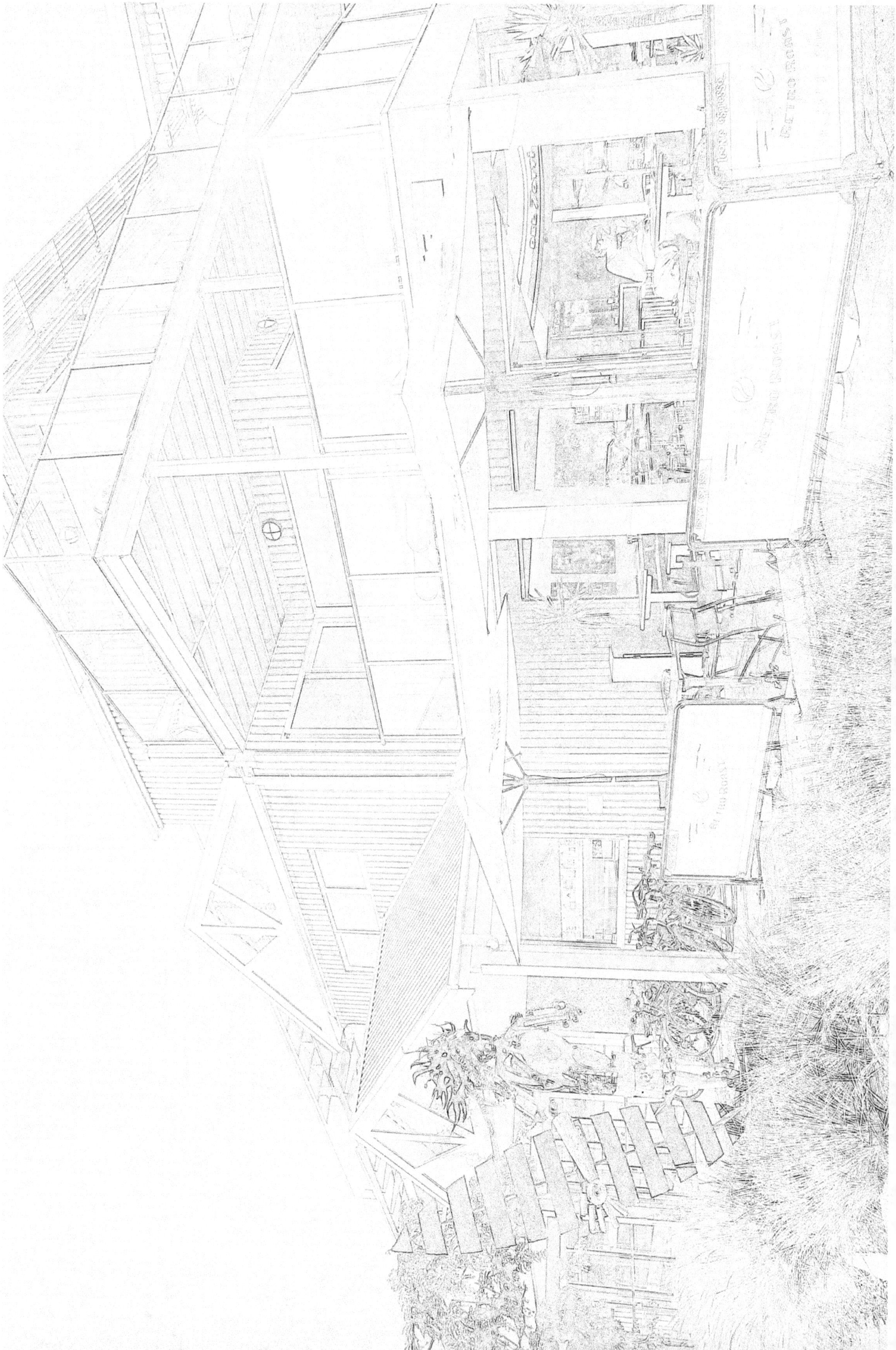

www.ingramcontent.com/pod-product-compliance
Lightning Source LLC
Chambersburg PA
CBHW081051180526
45170CB00005B/1756
* 9 7 8 0 3 5 9 8 2 3 3 6 9 *